Law Essentials

MEDIA LAW

Law Essentials

MEDIA LAW

Douglas Maule, M.A., LL.B.

and

Zhongdong Niu, LL.B., LL.M.

Lecturers in Law, Edinburgh Napier University

DUNDEE UNIVERSITY PRESS
2010

First edition published in Great Britain in 2009 by
Dundee University Press
University of Dundee
Dundee DD1 4HN

www.dup.dundee.ac.uk

Reprinted with corrections 2010

ISBN 978 1 84586 079 0

No natural forests were destroyed to make this product; only farmed timber was used
and replanted.

British Library Cataloguing-in-Publication Data
A catalogue record for this book is available on request from the British Library

Typeset by Waverley Typesetters, Warham, Norfolk
Printed and bound by Bell & Bain Ltd, Glasgow

CONTENTS

TABLE OF CASES

TABLE OF STATUTES

1 SOURCES OF THE LAW AND COURT STRUCTURE

SOURCES

Statutory law

Law has either a statutory or a common law source. Statutory law derives from the statutes of the Westminster Parliament, the Scottish Parliament, delegated legislation and the European Union.

Acts of the UK Parliament are known as "primary legislation" and may apply to the whole of the UK or only to parts of it. If an Act applies to Scotland only then the word "Scotland" will appear in brackets after the title. UK parliamentary legislation is in principle more powerful than law created by other sources of law and this is because of the doctrine known as "parliamentary supremacy".

All existing and future law must be consistent with, and interpreted in accordance with, the European Convention on Human Rights and European Community law, subject to certain provisos. Acts of the Scottish Parliament are made under powers delegated to the Scottish Parliament by the UK Parliament under the Scotland Act 1998.

Delegated legislation is secondary legislation and is made by members of the UK Government and the Scottish Executive under powers delegated to them by the UK Parliament or the Scottish Parliament.

Other government bodies such as local authorities have powers delegated to them by the UK Parliament. The validity of such legislation is dependent upon it falling within the perimeters set by the enabling UK Parliament or Scottish Parliament legislation.

Delegated legislation takes the form of statutory instruments, Scottish statutory instruments, bylaws etc. Courts also have power to make rules of procedure under powers delegated to them by government.

Common law

"Judicial precedent" or "case law" refers to rules created by courts and not by Parliament or any other legislature. It is found in cases decided by the courts and contained in law reports. The case must have been decided in a court of higher status in order for it to be binding on lower courts. For example, a decision in the House of Lords will bind all lower courts. The decisions of the House of Lords are not, however, binding on itself. The decisions of the Inner House of the Court of Session bind the Outer House and the sheriff court but not vice versa. The decisions of the latter two courts are not binding but may be persuasive. This means that other courts will take the decisions into account but will not be bound by them.

Judicial decisions from other countries (for example, Commonwealth countries) may assist interpretation but are not binding on our courts. However, decisions from the European Court of Justice must be followed. What is binding is called the "*ratio decidendi*" – that is to say, the reasoning behind the decision.

The decision of the higher court must also be in point, ie dealing with the same point of law. The principle underlying judicial precedent is consistency.

It is possible to alter these rules but it is a slow process through case law and legislation tends to be the preferred route.

Equity

In interpreting the law, the courts may also take account of the concept of equity and in Scotland this is mainly the function of the *nobile officium*. This is the equitable power of the Court of Session and the High Court of Justiciary to declare certain actions to be unlawful or to give a remedy where none is otherwise available.

Other sources

(a) Prerogative legislation

Certain powers of the Crown are now exercised by the Government. These are powers which were left to the Crown following the Glorious Revolution of 1688–89 and are referred to as the "Royal Prerogative". The powers are mostly executive (meaning that the Government exercises them) but some powers are legislative. This type of legislation is contained in, for example, Orders in Council. An example of this would be declarations of war.

(b) Institutional works

Originally influenced by Roman law, these are writings of certain authors, for example Viscount Stair's *Institutions of the Law of Scotland* (1681) which, at least from the mid-19th century, have been treated as authoritative by the courts where no clear legislation or case law is available.

(c) Custom

In essence, a custom is binding without the necessity for judicial recognition. Custom is not as important as a source of law as it was historically. Many customs have been either recognised in institutional works or incorporated into the common law (for example, in relation to succession).

It is, however, still possible to establish a custom as a new rule of law if certain criteria – as laid down by precedent - are met, although express judicial recognition of a custom is rare.

(d) Sources of EU law

Articles of the founding treaties are considered as primary legislation and Regulations, Directives and Decisions secondary legislation.

Regulations are directly applicable in the UK and become part of UK law immediately, without further process.

Directives are not directly applicable and require the UK legislative process to incorporate them into UK law. Directives therefore set out objectives and each Member State then has to implement the objectives, usually by way of an Act of Parliament. Usually a Member State has 2 years in which to cimplement the Directive.

Decisions are addressed to particular Member States or indeed individuals or corporate bodies. They are most often found where, for example, a Member State is in breach of competition policy.

CRIMINAL COURTS

There are three criminal courts in Scotland. They are the justice of the peace court; the sheriff court; and the High Court of Justiciary. Prosecutions in the justice of the peace court and the sheriff court are carried out by the procurator fiscal. In the High Court the prosecution is usually by an advocate-depute, although in very serious or important cases it can be undertaken by the Lord Advocate or the Solicitor General. Two types of procedure are used in criminal courts. The first is summary procedure which is used in the prosecution of less serious crimes and offences and in which there is no jury. The second is solemn procedure which is used to prosecute more serious crimes and offences and trial is before both a judge and a jury.

Prosecution in the High Court is by way of solemn procedure. The sheriff court hears cases under both summary and solemn procedure whereas in the justice of the peace courts there are only summary prosecutions.

Justice of the peace court

The justice of the peace courts were set up under the Criminal Proceedings etc (Reform) (Scotland) Act 2007 and are gradually replacing the old district courts which are being phased out. They are the summary courts with no juries and they deal with only less serious offences such as minor assaults and breaches of the peace. The judges are called "justices of the peace" and are not usually legally qualified or full time but have to undertake rigorous training. (Glasgow has stipendiary magistrates with similar sentencing powers to those of sheriffs.)

Justice of the peace courts, unlike the old district courts, are no longer administered by local authorities but by a sheriff principal. The court has territorial jurisdiction in respect of offences committed within:

(a) the sheriff court district in which it is located; and

(b) any other district in the same sheriffdom.

The clerk of court has to be a solicitor or advocate who advises the justice of the peace on legal matters.

Sentencing powers are limited to 60 days' imprisonment or a £2,500 fine. The Scottish Ministers have power to increase these limits by the issue of an appropriate order.

The prosecutor is the procurator fiscal and there is an appeal to the High Court against the justice of the peace's decision.

Sheriff court

Scotland is divided into six sheriffdoms and each sheriffdom is again divided into sheriff court districts. For example, the sheriffdom of Lothian and Borders is divided into the sheriff court districts of Edinburgh, Haddington, Jedburgh, Duns, Selkirk, Peebles and Linlithgow. A sheriff court only has jurisdiction to hear a case where the offence has been committed within the sheriff court district. It cannot hear cases involving murder, rape, treason and other cases of extreme seriousness reserved for the High Court, and those that, by statute, have to be prosecuted in the justice of the peace court.

The sheriff court hears both summary and solemn procedure cases, as well as civil actions. In summary prosecutions the sheriff sits alone and in solemn cases there is a jury of 15 members of the public.

All sheriffs are legally qualified and must be an advocate or solicitor of experience. Each sheriff court has at least one sheriff but the busier courts may have a number of sheriffs.

A sheriff principal is in charge of the administration of every sheriffdom. The sheriff principal will hear appeals in civil cases and occasionally will sit as a trial judge in criminal prosecutions.

The clerk of court, who works for the Scottish Court Service, is not legally qualified, and is known as the "sheriff clerk" (assisted by deputes). In summary proceedings there is a maximum fine of £10,000 and the maximum prison sentence is for 12 months. In solemn cases the power to fine is unlimited (unless restricted by statute), and there is a maximum prison sentence of 5 years. A sheriff may send an accused to the High Court for sentencing where he is of the opinion that a longer prison sentence would be appropriate.

All solemn procedure cases are commenced in the sheriff court, including murder and rape. A solemn case is commenced when the accused appears in front of a sheriff on petition. The sheriff will then decide whether to remand the accused or release him on bail.

There are two youth courts (in Airdrie and Hamilton Sheriff Courts) which deal with persistent offenders aged from 17 to 19. Special Drugs Courts were also introduced in 2001 for offenders over the age of 21 and with the aim of reducing the number of drug-related offences. There are presently three such courts (in Glasgow, Dunfermline and Kirkcaldy).

High Court

The High Court of Justiciary was established in 1672 and is a court of both first and second instance. It therefore hears cases for the first time (trial) and also sits as a court of appeal. The High Court is the supreme criminal court in Scotland and there is no appeal from it unless the case relates to a devolution issue where there is an appeal to the Judicial Committee of the Privy Council.

It is presided over by the Lord Justice-General who is assisted by the second most senior judge who is called the "Lord Justice-Clerk". The other judges are known as "Lords Commissioners of Justiciary".

The High Court, when not an appeal court, goes on circuit and sits in various locations around Scotland, for example Dundee, Inverness and Aberdeen, but sits permanently in Glasgow and Edinburgh.

Usually the court will consist of a judge and a jury of 15 but in important complex cases there may be three judges.

The High Court has jurisdiction over the whole of Scotland and its territorial waters. It only hears the most serious cases and has sole jurisdiction over murder, rape, treason and breach of duty by magistrates (s 3(6) of the Criminal Procedure (Scotland) Act 1995).

There is no limit on sentencing for common law crimes which can be for life imprisonment and unlimited fine. An offence that is statutory may impose a limit.

The prosecutors in the High Court are called "advocates depute"; they assist the Lord Advocate who is in charge of the prosecution of crime in Scotland.

Only advocates or solicitor-advocates are allowed to appear in the High Court. As an appeal court; the High Court hears appeals from the High Court sitting as a court of first instance, the sheriff court and the justice of the peace court. There are two types of appeal: summary appeals (justiciary roll) and solemn appeals. Appeals are on points of law only since only the trial court of the first instance can properly assess the credibility and reliability of the facts. It can, in exceptional circumstances, consider new evidence where such evidence was not known or available at the trial court. At least three judges sit at an appeal, although this may be increased in important cases.

Declaratory power (nobile officium)

This is an equitable power given to the High Court of Justiciary (and the Court of Session) where the court may give a remedy where no other exists, or declare a certain act to be criminal. However, there may be some doubt about this as a result of the implementation of the Human Rights Act 1998. It is used in contempt of court cases where there is no right of appeal.

CRIMINAL PROCEDURE

There are two types of criminal procedure in Scotland. Solemn procedure is used in the sheriff courts and the High Court; summary procedure is used in the sheriff and the justice of the peace courts.

Solemn procedure

The petition

Solemn procedure cases are initiated in the sheriff court. This is done by the presentation to the sheriff of a document called a petition. The petition is a request by the procurator fiscal to commit the accused to prison until liberated in due course of law. Note that the charges in the petition may not be the same as the charges in the indictment. For example, a charge of assault may later become a charge of murder where the victim dies.

First examination

The accused's first appearance on petition is always in the sheriff court, even although the trial may take place in the High Court.

The hearing before the sheriff is known as the "first examination" and takes place in private in the sheriff's chambers. Very often this hearing is purely formal and lasts only a few minutes. The accused will usually make "no plea or declaration". The Press are therefore not admitted.

Note that the plea is not a plea of "guilty" or "not guilty". The accused has not yet been served with the final charges which are contained in a document called the "indictment". The procurator fiscal may then ask the sheriff to commit the accused fully ("full committal" means remand in prison until liberated in due course of law unless bail is granted. Bail is applied for at this stage if appropriate). Sometimes the procurator fiscal will ask for a committal for further examination where, for example, the fiscal wishes to make further enquiries.

Further examination

If the accused has been committed for further examination, the second hearing must take place within 8 days and the accused must then be fully committed or released on bail.

Judicial examination

The judicial examination is part of the petition procedure. The judicial examination is a separate hearing held in private before a sheriff and the Press are not allowed to attend.

The purpose of the examination is to allow the procurator fiscal to find out whether the accused admits or denies the charge or whether he has any explanation or defence or anything to say by way of explanation regarding any confession he may have made.

Procedure under s 76 of the Criminal Procedure (Scotland) Act 1995

There is provision under the above section for the accused to plead guilty at an early stage. The accused sends a standard form letter to the procurator fiscal, intimating that he wishes to plead guilty. The fiscal then prepares a shortened form of the indictment and serves it on the accused. The accused will then enter a plea of guilty to the court at an accelerated diet (hearing).

Preliminary hearing

In High Court trials a preliminary hearing will then be fixed. At this hearing the Crown and the defence have to lodge a written record setting out their state of preparedness. In the sheriff court there is a first diet at which the accused enters a plea.

The Crown precognition

Where the accused has been fully committed then the fiscal prepares the Crown precognition. This is done by taking statements from all the prosecution witnesses and binding them up into volumes together with a list of productions, any transcript of any interviews or of any judicial examination, any previous convictions, a list of witnesses and a short introductory report on the case. This bound volume is known as the Crown precognition.

The fiscal then sends the bound precognition to the Crown Office in Edinburgh. The advocates-depute look at the case and send back instructions to the fiscal on how to proceed if the case is to be heard in the sheriff court (eg "do not proceed", or "proceed in sheriff court on assault charge in front of a sheriff and jury", or "proceed in the High Court". Advice may also be given on the form of the charges in the indictment).

Where it is decided to proceed in the High Court then the indictment (the document that contains the final charges against the accused) will be prepared by an advocate-depute. Otherwise the fiscal prepares the indictment, as instructed by the Crown Office.

Preliminary hearing on the indictment

In sheriff court cases there is a first diet where the court finds out whether the trial is likely to proceed. The court is concerned whether both prosecutor and defence are prepared for the trial. The indictment must be served at least 15 days before this. In High Court cases it must be served at least 29 days before the preliminary hearing. At the time of service of the indictment, the indictment is served with a copy of the productions and a list of the Crown witnesses and of any schedule of previous convictions. The defence lawyers will then take statements from the witnesses. It is part of the right of the accused to a fair trial that all the Crown witnesses can be precognosed by the defence solicitor (Human Rights Act 1998, Sch 1, Pt I, Art 6(3)(d)). This is often referred to as the "fair notice" rule.

Any special defences (such as alibi) must be intimated to the Crown at least 7 days prior to the commencement of the preliminary hearing or, in the sheriff court, at or before the first diet. This is so that the Crown has fair notice of the defence and can therefore carry out its own investigations into it defence and precognose the witnesses who may speak to the defence.

The trial

Where the accused has pleaded "not guilty", the jury will be empanelled.

The names of all persons summoned to appear on jury duty will be placed in a bowl and the clerk of court will pick 15 names at random. Up until 1995 there was a right to object to three jurors without giving a reason. It is still possible to object to any juror but there must be a good reason for this (eg the juror knows the accused or knows about the crime).

The jury is then sworn in and the indictment and any special defence are read out to the jury. The trial will then commence with the calling of the first prosecution witness. The prosecution always leads evidence first. Note that in Scotland there are no opening speeches.

Examination of witnesses The examination of each witness starts with the taking of the witnesses evidence by the party calling them to give evidence (this is known as "examination in chief") and during this examination no leading questions can be asked. "Leading questions" are those which suggest the answer the questioner seeks to be given.

This is followed by cross-examination by the defence. The aim of cross-examination is to test the evidence that has been given, to obtain any qualifications to it, and to put to the witness the case of the party who did not call the witness to give evidence. These questions can be leading.

There may be a re-examination by the party who first called the witness where clarification is required about the answers made under cross-examination or where it is necessary to clarify or contradict some fresh evidence brought out in the cross-examination.

At the end of the Crown case the defence may be of the opinion that there is insufficient evidence to convict. Where this happens the defence may put before the judge a submission that there is no case to answer. This submission is done outwith the presence of the jury. If the submission is successful the trial will come to an end and the accused is pronounced "not guilty" on the charge.

In Scotland there is a rule, called the "corroboration rule", which states that evidence of the crucial facts (that the crime was committed and that the accused committed the crime) must come from two independent sources. This acts as a very important check on the proof of those crucial facts. Insufficient evidence will usually occur only where one or both of the crucial facts is not corroborated.

If there is not a "no case to answer" submission or if such a submission is unsuccessful then the trial will continue.

Reporting Note that, from a reporting point of view, where the submission is not successful care should be taken not to report this at the time, as the jury will not have heard the submission and must not be influenced by any information about the trial other than from evidence they have heard in court.

This restriction on reporting also applies where there is an objection to particular evidence in the trial. Evidence may inadmissible because of a rule of evidence (eg if it was obtained unfairly or is prejudicial). Such objections are also heard outwith the presence of the jury members so as not to influence them.

Defence case If the trial continues, then at the end of the prosecution case the defence will go through a similar procedure with the defence witnesses (examination in chief, cross-examination and re-examination, as before).

Note that the defence does not have to lead any evidence. It is up to the Crown to prove the facts of the case to the satisfaction of the jury, to the standard of "beyond reasonable doubt". (This burden of proof is on the Crown throughout and so the defence doesn't have to prove anything. Often the strategy of the defence is simply to test the Crown case and not to put an opposing case of its own.)

Closing speeches At the conclusion of the defence case the prosecution will then be asked to make a closing speech to the jury, summing up the case for the prosecution. This is then followed by the defence closing speech.

Charge to the jury Finally, the judge will then address the jury members, advising them of the appropriate law which they must apply (because the judge is the "master of the law"). He will also advise them of the standard of proof. The jury are the masters of the facts. It is up to them to consider which evidence they believe and which they reject; what weight to give to the evidence they have heard; what inferences they think should be drawn from the evidence they have heard; and whether they consider that the evidence raises any reasonable doubt as to the accused's guilt. This speech is called the judge's "charge to the jury".

Verdict   The jury will then usually retire to elect a foreman and consider the verdict. It is important to remember that the Press must at no point talk to any member of the jury.

In Scotland there are three possible verdicts:

(1) guilty;

(2) not guilty;

(3) not proven.

When it has reached its verdict the jury returns to the court; the clerk of court will ask the foreman whether the jury has reached a verdict. If it has, the clerk will ask whether it is a unanimous or a majority verdict (a majority verdict means that there must be at least eight members of the jury who have voted for a verdict).

If the verdict is "not guilty" or "not proven", the accused is released. Both of these verdicts are verdicts of acquittal. "Not guilty" is more emphatic than "not proven". Usually, a "not proven" verdict will occur where there has been a problem with the quantity or quality of the evidence.

If the verdict is "guilty" then the prosecutor will move for sentence and produce any schedule of previous convictions. The lawyer for the defence will then address the court by giving a plea in mitigation of sentence and also the personal circumstances of the accused. The judge will then pass sentence. Very often, before sentence, it is necessary to obtain social work or other reports in order that the sentence given by the judge takes these matters into account.

Summary procedure

This procedure is used in the sheriff courts and the justice of the peace courts and trial is by judge only.

Prosecutions are carried out by the procurator fiscal. Initially, the police send a report to the fiscal who will then decide whether to prosecute and, if so, in which court.

Where it is decided to prosecute there is no initial stage (petition stage) as in solemn proceedings. The fiscal will prepare a document called the "complaint" (the equivalent of the indictment in solemn proceedings). This contains the final charges against the accused. The fiscal will then have the complaint served on the accused and cite the accused to answer the complaint on a particular day. Answering can be done by:

(1) attending court;

(2) arranging for a lawyer to attend;

(3) writing to the court using a reply form.

Where the accused has been arrested and is being held in custody, he must appear on the next court day. The complaint is served on the accused in the police cells, usually situated below the court.

Pleading diet   The first court hearing (diet) is called the pleading diet. At this, the accused will enter a plea of "guilty" or "not guilty". "Guilty" pleas are usually dealt with straight away. Where the plea is "not guilty" the court will fix a date for the trial and if the accused is in custody the question of bail will be dealt with.

In summary cases the fiscal does not take statements from the prosecution witnesses but will usually rely on police statements copied from police notebooks. The police attending an incident will take statements from witnesses who are at the scene. Usually these will be answers given to the police in response to their questions. The actual questions are, however, usually not recorded in the notebooks.

The defence agent will obtain a list of the prosecution witnesses and take statements from them directly.

Intermediate diet   There is usually an intermediate diet to find out the state of preparation of the parties, whether any evidence has been agreed and whether the accused still wishes to go to trial or has decided to plead guilty.

The trial   A lot of cases are usually set down for trial on a particular day. As a result, there is usually a "call-over" of trials to fix a time and, where there is more than one courtroom, which court will be used for each trial.

Special defences

These are intimated to the prosecutor at the intermediate diet or 10 days before the trial. Again, the aim is that fair notice of the defence be given to the prosecutor.

Trial procedure

There are no juries in summary trials: the procedure is very similar to that of a solemn procedure trial. Crown witnesses are examined first, followed by the defence witnesses. Both parties then sum up and the judge will then reach a verdict. The accused will be either released or sentenced.

Appeals

Solemn procedure

A person convicted under solemn procedure can appeal against conviction, sentence or both. An appeal is based on an alleged miscarriage of justice. In solemn cases the prosecution can also appeal against leniency of a sentence.

Under the Criminal Procedure (Scotland) Act 1995, an appeal can proceed only where leave to appeal has been granted. To obtain leave, the appeal grounds are considered by a High Court judge alone, without the parties present. This is sometimes referred to as the "sift".

Where leave to appeal is refused, the applicant can make a second application which is considered by three judges.

The appeal is based on a written notice of appeal setting out the grounds for the appeal and a report by the trial judge on the case generally and on the grounds for appeal.

Very occasionally, the appeal court can hear new evidence where this was not available at the time of the trial and there is a reasonable explanation as to why it was not heard at the trial.

The appeal court can:

- affirm the verdict of the original court;
- set aside the verdict and quash the conviction;
- set aside the verdict and authorise a fresh trial;
- affirm a sentence;
- quash the sentence and pass another sentence (which can be more severe than the original sentence).

Summary procedure

Appeal can be against sentence or conviction or both – again, on the ground of a miscarriage of justice. The prosecutor can appeal against undue leniency or acquittal on a point of law. Leave to appeal is required as in solemn cases.

Appeal is by way of stated case. Application for a stated case must be made within 1 week of sentence (s 176 of the Criminal Procedure (Scotland) Act 1995). The High Court can, *inter alia*:

- send the case back to the original court, with instructions on how to proceed;
- affirm the verdict or set aside the verdict and quash the conviction;
- reduce or increase a sentence or grant authority for a new prosecution.

Bill of suspension

This form of appeal is used only where there has been some sort of irregularity in the trial proceedings.

Special defences

The following are special defences:

- *Alibi*. The accused maintains that he was at some other place at the time when and place where the crime was committed.
- *Incrimination/impeachment*. The accused alleges that some other named person committed the crime.
- *Self-defence*. The accused alleges that he was defending himself or a third party from attack.
- *Insanity*. The accused alleges that at the time of the crime he was suffering from some mental disorder.
- *Automatism*. The accused alleges that he could not have intended to commit the crime because, through no fault of his own, he was under the influence of some external factor (eg drugs) and was therefore not aware of or in control of the situation at the time of the crime. Automatism is not a defence where it is self-induced.
- *Coercion or necessity*. This is where the accused alleges that he was forced to commit the crime.

Pleas in bar of trial

A successful plea in bar of trial means that the trial will not take place at a particular time, or at all.

The following are pleas in bar of trial:

(1) Insanity at the time of the trial (so that the accused is unable to understand the nature of court proceedings or to instruct a solicitor or advocate to represent him).

(2) The accused has "tholed his assize", ie he has already stood trial for the same crime.

(3) The accused has given evidence for the Crown in the trial of another person on the same charge ("Queen's evidence").

(4) Excessive delay in bringing the accused to trial (so that some time limit is breached or the events occurred so long ago that memories have faded and the evidence of witnesses is unlikely to remain reliable).

(5) Unfair pre-trial publicity.

(6) Non-age: no child under the age of 8 years can be prosecuted.

Restrictions against undue delay

There is a general principle in Scotland that an accused person must be brought to trial as soon as possible, so as to prevent detention for long periods of time without trial, or, where he is not detained, so as to prevent oppression as a result of delay. In Scotland the rules are mainly statutory.

Solemn procedure

12- and 11-month rules   These rules apply where the accused is *not* in custody awaiting trial. Where an indictment has been served on the accused the preliminary hearing must take place within 11 months and in any event the trial must commence within 12 months. If this does not happen then the accused must be discharged and is free from further prosecution. The 12- and 11-month periods can be extended where sufficient reason is given. Fault on the part of the Crown will not usually be sufficient reason.

80-day rule   Where an accused has been fully committed for trial in custody (bail has not been granted) then the indictment has to be served within 80 days from the time of committal. This means that the accused is entitled to bail if it is not served within the 80-day period. Note that this does not mean that the prosecution will fall.

110- and 140-day rules   Under these rules, where the accused is in custody and an indictment has been served, a preliminary hearing must be commenced within 110 days or the accused is entitled to be admitted to bail. The trial must commence within 140 days or the accused is entitled to be admitted to bail.

Summary procedure

6-month rule   In statutory offences the general rule is that proceedings must be commenced within 6 months after the commission of the offence.

40-day rule   Where an accused is in custody awaiting trial, the trial must commence within 40 days from the day after the complaint is brought in court. If it does not commence within those 40 days, the accused must be liberated and is free from further prosecution. Again, the 40-day period can be extended where good cause is shown.

Bail

The principle underlying bail is that an accused is presumed innocent until proven guilty. There must therefore be a very good reason to deprive a person of his liberty while awaiting trial.

Bail is now regulated by the Criminal Procedure (Scotland) Act 1995 (as amended), the Bail, Judicial Appointments etc (Scotland) Act 2000 and the Criminal Proceedings etc (Reform) (Scotland) Act 2007.

The system of monetary bail was abolished in 1980, although a pledge of money can still be imposed as a condition of bail (but this is probably no longer used).

Prior to the passing of the Bail, Judicial Appointments etc (Scotland) Act 2000, bail was not available where the charge was murder or treason or where the accused had already been convicted of rape or culpable homicide. Now, all accused persons where they are held in custody can apply for bail irrespective of the crime or offence with which they have been charged.

Bail is dealt with at the first examination in solemn proceedings or at the pleading diet in summary proceedings and must be determined by the end of the day after the day on which the accused appeared before the judge.

The police can also grant bail in summary cases, on an undertaking to appear in court when required.

Instead of money bail, the court will usually grant a bail order which contains standard bail conditions:

(1) that the accused will appear at every court hearing when required;

(2) that he will not commit an offence while on bail;

(3) that he will not interfere with witnesses;

(4) that he will make himself available to allow enquiries to be made or for the preparation of reports;

The court can impose further conditions if required, for example that the accused must surrender his passport.

Refusal or granting of bail

The judge has to balance the presumption of innocence with the seriousness of the crime, the previous record of the accused, the likelihood of justice being frustrated if the accused is released, and the safety of the public. The various criteria on which the judge must decide are statutory. The judge must give reasons for granting or refusing bail. There is a right of appeal to the High Court against the refusal or the granting of bail which appeal is heard in private before one judge.

Where an accused commits a further offence while subject to a bail order, the court will take this into account when sentencing the accused for the offence.

Reporting

Bail hearings are usually held in private in solemn proceedings and appeals. In summary cases, the hearing will be in open court.

Any previous convictions that may be discussed at a bail hearing should not be published, as is the case generally for any information that might prejudice the proceedings.

CIVIL COURTS

Most civil cases involve actions between legal persons, for example individuals, companies or partnerships. They are raised by one party (known as the "pursuer") against another party (known as the "defender"). Actions for payment, divorce, breach of contract, or reparation are all examples of civil actions. The onus of proof is usually on the person raising the action and the decision as to whether the case has been proved or not is on the balance of probabilities.

Three courts have jurisdiction to hear civil cases:

- the sheriff court;
- the Court of Session;
- the Supreme Court of the United Kingdom.

The sheriff court

The sheriff court hears both civil and criminal proceedings. In civil actions the court has jurisdiction where the defender resides within the sheriff court district and has done so for at least 40 days, or has a place of business there. Jurisdiction can also be founded in other circumstances, for example if a contract was performed there. The sheriff court can hear most types of civil action but has sole jurisdiction to hear small claim and summary cause actions.

Small claims procedure is used where the amount sued for is under £3,000. It is a simplified procedure using pre-printed forms and the aim is to make it cheap, quick and informal to use. Lawyers are often not involved and the costs are restricted. There is an appeal to the sheriff principal on a point of law.

Actions for over £3,000 and up to £5,000 are heard in a summary cause court. Although the procedure there is more formal than in the small claims court, there are no written pleadings. The pursuer fills in a pre-printed form which is served on the defender who then completes a defences section. Thereafter there is a hearing called a "proof", at which the parties lead evidence before the sheriff.

An appeal on a point of law can be made to the sheriff principal and thereafter to the Inner House of the Court of Session where leave to appeal is granted.

Actions for sums over £5,000, and other types of sheriff court proceedings such as actions for divorce, are called "ordinary cause actions". They are commenced by serving a document called an "initial writ" on the defender, setting out the pursuer's claim. The defender has to intimate that the action is to be defended and then lodge defences to the claim within a certain period of time. Both parties then adjust their pleadings in a document called the "open record". Once the period of adjustment is over, the sheriff will close the record and no further alterations are allowed unless permitted by the court. A date for a proof will then be fixed or, if there are any pleas in law to the relevancy or lack of specification in the pleadings by either party, the sheriff will set a date for a debate or proof before answer. A plea to the relevancy or specification can be made by either party to the action. For example, if the averments or facts set out in the pleadings are insufficient to justify a particular defence or, conversely, are insufficient to support the claim by the pursuer, then the action may be dismissed or decree may be granted. A debate takes place before any evidence is heard at a proof. In a proof before answer, evidence is heard at the proof and the question of relevancy is considered after this.

An appeal against a sheriff's decision lies to the sheriff principal and then to the Inner House of the Court of Session.

Court of Session

Outer House and Inner House

The Court of Session is divided into two parts. The Outer House is a court of first instance (hearing cases for the first time) and the Inner House is a court of appeal. Both courts have jurisdiction over the whole of Scotland and sit in Edinburgh.

The judges in the Court of Session are called "Senators of the College of Justice" and are also known as "Lords of Council and Session". The most senior judge is the Lord President and the second senior judge is the Lord Justice-Clerk.

The Court of Session has sole jurisdiction to hear actions for the reduction of documents, actions relating to personal status, actions to prove the tenor of documents and petitions for the winding-up of certain companies. It can also review the administrative decisions of bodies such as local authorities and Government Ministers.

Proceedings raised in the Outer House are usually heard before a judge sitting alone, who is referred to as a "Lord Ordinary". It is still possible to have jury trials in the Court of Session, in personal injury cases. A jury consists of 12 members of the public in civil actions, as opposed to 15 in criminal cases. (Civil jury trials in the sheriff court were abolished a number of years ago.)

The procedure followed in the Court of Session is very similar to that in sheriff court ordinary actions, except that proceedings are initiated by serving a summons on the defender as opposed to the initial writ used in ordinary actions.

The Inner House is an appeal court and is divided into two divisions each of equal status. The First Division comprises the Lord President and three other senior judges and the Second Division is headed by the Lord Justice-Clerk and three other senior judges. Usually an appeal will be heard by three judges but this number can be increased in important and complex cases. Appeals on points of law are made to the Inner House from the Outer House, the sheriff court and tribunals such as an employment tribunals.

Supreme Court of the United Kingdom

The Judicial Committee of the House of Lords formerly heard appeals from the Inner House of the Court of Session. It was the final court of appeal for civil actions in Scotland. The judges were known as "Lords of Appeal in Ordinary" and, by convention, two were Scottish. Usually a Bench of five Lords of Appeal would sit to hear an appeal. Under the Constitutional Reform Act 2005, the appellate jurisdiction of the House of Lords has been transferred to the Supreme Court for the United Kingdom with effect from 1 October 2009.

2 REPORTING RESTRICTIONS

CHILDREN INVOLVED IN CRIMINAL PROCEEDINGS

Children can be prosecuted from the age of 8 years, although there are proposals to increase the age of criminal liability to 12. A child will face prosecution only for serious offences or crimes such as murder or rape and most criminal cases involving children are referred to a children's hearing instead.

Under s 42(1) of the Criminal Procedure (Scotland) Act 1995, "No child under the age of 16 years shall be prosecuted for any offence except on the instructions of the Lord Advocate, or at his instance; and no court other than the High Court and the sheriff court shall have jurisdiction over a child under the age of 16 years for an offence".

Section 50 of the 1995 Act prohibits any child under the age of 14 from being present in court during proceedings unless required as a witness. A judge can also clear the court to hear the evidence of a child in cases involving immorality or indecency, although *bona fide* members of the Press are permitted to stay for reporting purposes. The Vulnerable Witnesses (Scotland) Act 2004 permits persons under the age of 16 years who are witnesses to give evidence provided for by special means, for example TV link or screen. Children under 12 may not have to give evidence in the court building at all.

Reporting of criminal proceedings involving children

Section 47(1) of the Criminal Procedure (Scotland) Act 1995 prohibits any newspaper, television or radio report of any proceedings from revealing the name, address or school, or including any particulars calculated to lead to the identification, of any person under the age of 16 concerned in the proceedings. This applies where the person under 16 is the accused, the victim or a witness. Under s 47(2), no picture of the person under 16 or any picture including the person can be published. The section does not apply to children who are dead.

There is an exception to the ban on identification under s 47(4) where the person under 16 is a witness only and no one against whom the proceedings are taken is under 16, unless the court makes an order preventing identification.

The court can dispense with the ban on identification at any time during the proceedings, to the extent that it specifies, where it is satisfied that it is in the public interest to do so. The First Minister has similar powers at the end of the proceedings to lift the ban in the public interest.

"Jigsaw" identification

There is a possibility of identifying a child in cases where he is the victim of incest or has been the subject of some other sort of sexual or domestic abuse. This can occur where the facts from more than one report are put together and result in what is known as "jigsaw" identification. Therefore in reporting these types of cases the usual practice is to name the accused and refer to the crime as "a serious sexual offence against a child". No reference is made to the relationship between the child and the accused.

CHILDREN'S HEARINGS

Children's hearings were introduced by the Social Work (Scotland) Act 1968 and replaced the previous system which used juvenile courts. One of the main purposes of the new system was to remove children as far as possible from the criminal court system and focus on the child's welfare rather than punishment. Children's hearings are not concerned solely with criminal behaviour but also with many other issues involving children such as abuse, truancy and lack of parental control. For the purposes of a children's hearing a "child" means a person under the age of 16 or, where the child is already subject to a supervision order, 18. The Children (Scotland) Act 1995 has, for the most part, replaced the provisions of the 1968 Act. It requires all local government areas to establish a children's panel to hear cases referred to a children's hearing. To do this they also have to set up a children's panel advisory committee which then recommends the appointment of suitable persons to the panel. Once appointed, members of a panel receive rigorous training. A children's hearing comprises a chairman and two other members of the panel. There must be at least one man and one woman hearing the case.

The person who decides whether or not to refer a case to a children's hearing is called a reporter. Reporters are not now employed by local authorities but by the Scottish Reporters Administration and they need not be legally qualified.

When a reporter receives information (this can be from many sources such as from the police, a member of the public or a social work department) that a children's hearing may be required, he must carry out an initial investigation. Having completed the investigation and before referring the case, the reporter must be satisfied that:

(1) at least one of the grounds of referral has been satisfied under s 52(2) of the Children (Scotland) Act 1995; and

(2) the child is in need of compulsory measures of supervision.

There are various grounds for referral under s 52(2) and, as mentioned above, they are not limited to criminal offences. For example, a child can be referred where he is beyond parental control or is the victim of an offence, or is not attending school.

The hearing itself is in private (although a relevant person, usually a person with parental responsibilities, has a right to attend), but under s 43(3)(b) of the 1995 Act "a *bona fide* representative of a newspaper or news agency" can attend. However, this is subject to s 43(4) which provides that the children's hearing can exclude the Press, or other persons including parents, where it is satisfied that:

(a) it is necessary to do so, in the interests of the child, in order to obtain the child's views in relation to the case before the hearing; or

(b) the presence of that person is causing, or is likely to cause, significant distress to the child.

The chairman may, after that exclusion has ended, give an explanation of the substance of what took place at the hearing.

The proceedings at a children's hearing are informal. The hearing has to consider whether a safeguarder should be appointed to represent the interests of the child. Legal aid is now available in certain cases.

The chairman is required to explain the grounds of referral and must then establish whether they have been accepted. If they are not accepted then an application must be made to the sheriff court for the sheriff to establish whether the grounds have been proved. If the sheriff finds that they are established, after an informal hearing where evidence is led by both parties, the case is sent back to the children's hearing for disposal. The sheriff has discretion to allow the Press in to report the proceedings. Once the grounds for referral are either accepted or established by a sheriff, the hearing will then decide whether a supervision requirement is necessary.

An appeal against the decision of the hearing or the finding of a sheriff lies to the sheriff principal and then the Court of Session.

Under the Antisocial Behaviour (Scotland) Act 2004, which introduced ASBOs into Scotland for children, the court may require the reporter to bring the child before a hearing to decide whether to impose a supervision order.

Reporting restrictions relating to children's hearings

Any report of the proceedings of children's hearing, whether by newspaper, television or radio, must not include any information or photograph (even where the face of the child is blacked out) that might identify the child involved.

Under s 44 of the Children (Scotland) Act 1995 it is an offence to publish any matter which is intended to, or is likely to, identify any child concerned in a children's hearing, or the address or school of the child. The ban on identification also applies to proceedings before a sheriff and to any appeal. Reports of children's hearings published in England, Wales and Northern Ireland are also subject to this provision.

The prohibition also applies to sheriff court hearings dealing with child protection or exclusion orders.

The requirement that a publication does not identify a child may be dispensed with in the interests of justice, by the sheriff in proceedings before him, the Court of Session in any appeal, or by the First Minister where this is deemed appropriate.

There is a defence under s 5 of the Act if the accused can show that he did not know and had no reason to suspect that published matter was intended to, or was likely to, identify the child or his address or school.

FATAL ACCIDENT INQUIRIES

Fatal accident inquiries are held in the sheriff court, under the Fatal Accident and Sudden Deaths Inquiry (Scotland) Act 1976. They are public inquiries into fatal accidents at work and deaths in legal custody. They may also be held where the Lord Advocate considers it to be in the public interest where the death was suspicious, unexplained or occurred in circumstances which give rise to public concern. The sheriff has power under s 4 of the Act, either at his own instance or on application made to him by any party to the inquiry, to make an order in respect of any person under the age of 17 involved in the inquiry, provided that:

(a) no report of the inquiry which is made in a newspaper or other publication or a sound or television broadcast shall reveal the name, address or school, or include any particulars calculated to lead to the identification, of that person;

(b) no picture relating to the inquiry which is or includes a picture of that person shall be published in any newspaper or other publication or televised broadcast.

CLOSED DOORS

Usually court proceedings are held in public but there are circumstances, especially in cases involving sexual crimes, where the court will be cleared of all persons not actually involved in the proceedings. For example, in rape trials the woman alleging rape will usually give evidence behind closed doors.

Judges have power under s 92(3) of the Criminal Procedure (Scotland) Act 1995 to "clear a court from the commencement of the leading of evidence in a trial for rape or the like". The judge may "if he thinks fit, cause all persons other than the accused and counsel and solicitors to be removed from the court-room". Usually, members of the Press are permitted to remain, on the understanding that they do not identify the woman. Judges also have power under s 11 of the Contempt of Court Act 1981 to make an order prohibiting the publication of a name or other matter in connection with the proceedings before it in rape and other cases involving sexual offences.

JUDICIAL PROCEEDINGS (REGULATION OF REPORTS) ACT 1926

Section 1(a) of the 1926 Act provides for a general ban on the publishing, in relation to any judicial proceedings, of indecent material, including medical, surgical or physiological matters, "calculated to injure public morals".

The reporting of matrimonial proceedings is also regulated by the Act, although it is not for the protection of the parties involved in the divorce but to protect injury to public morals. The provisions of the Act are now somewhat out of date and prosecutions are extremely rare.

The maximum penalty for contravention of the Act is 4 months' imprisonment or a fine of £5,000, or both.

Matrimonial actions

The term "matrimonial" includes actions for divorce, judicial separation and nullity of marriage. Actions of judicial separation are rare but may be raised where the parties are opposed to divorce. Marriages can also be annulled on the basis that they were never valid and, again, these are fairly rare. Divorce actions can be raised either in the sheriff court or in the Court of Session. All such actions can be granted only on the ground of the irretrievable breakdown of the marriage. Where they are undefended they usually proceed by way of affidavit evidence which dispenses with the need to hear the evidence in court. A simplified procedure can be used if there are no children of the marriage under 16 years; neither party is seeking any financial provision; and the parties have been separated for 1 year (where both consent to the divorce) or 2 years (where there is no consent).

Under s 1(i)(b) of the Judicial Proceedings (Regulation of Reports) Act 1926, nothing may be published concerning actions of divorce, nullity of marriage, or judicial separation except:

(1) the names, addresses and occupations of the parties to the action and of any witnesses;

(2) a concise statement of the charges, counter-charges and defences in support of which evidence has been given;

(3) submissions on any points of law arising during the proceedings, including the court's decision on any legal point;

(4) the judgment of the court and any observations made by the judge in giving judgment.

In terms of the Act, apart from the names and addresses of the parties and witnesses, only a concise report of any charges (for example, adultery) or defences or counter-charges can be published and only when this has been supported by evidence given in court or by way of affidavit.

The Act allows the reporting of points of law (such as whether or not particular evidence is admissible) which may arise during the proceedings, and the court's decision thereon. Finally, because of the restrictions imposed by the Act, the media will often report the proceedings only at the point where the judge gives his decision. Usually a judge will not give a decision immediately but issue a written judgment at a later date. This can be used for the purpose of reporting the action.

Children

There is no general ban on the identification of children involved in civil proceedings, as there is for those involved in criminal ones. However, under s 46 of the Children and Young Persons (Scotland) Act 1937 (as amended), in relation to any proceedings before any court (whether civil or criminal), a judge may direct that no newspaper (or radio or television) report shall reveal the name, address or school, or include any particulars calculated to lead to the identification, of a person under 17 years who is concerned in the proceedings.

3 CONTEMPT OF COURT

INTRODUCTION

The law of contempt is concerned with the ability of courts in the UK to maintain their authority and deal with conduct that undermines their main function, which is the administration of justice. In *HM Advocate* v *Airs* (1975) contempt was defined as follows:

> "it is the name given to conduct which challenges or affronts the authority of the court or the supremacy of the law itself whether it takes place in or in connection with civil or criminal proceedings".

Lord Clyde stated in *Johnson* v *Grant* (1923) that:

> "The offence consists in interfering with the administration of the law; in impeding and perverting the course of justice ... it is not the dignity of the court which is offended ... it is the fundamental supremacy of the law which is challenged."

Contempt can be divided into various types or categories: for example, failure to carry out an order of the court or conduct that disrupts the proceedings before the court. This chapter, however, considers the ways in which the media can fall foul of the law of contempt. This category of contempt relates to communications which might potentially prejudice or impede court proceedings. Contempt of court, where it applies to prejudicial communications, is for the most part regulated not by the common law, as is the case with most of the other categories, but by the Contempt of Court Act 1981 (the "1981 Act").

Prejudicial coverage of legal proceedings by the media, where it is sufficiently serious, is recognised as being a plea in bar of trial which, if successful, can prevent a trial taking place at all. In Scotland this is a rare occurrence. (For an example of a plea in bar of trial on the basis of media prejudice, see *Haney* v *HM Advocate (No 2)* (2003).) It can also found grounds for moving a trial from one location to another or for an appeal against conviction.

JUDGES

All courts in Scotland have summary powers to ensure that conduct which interferes with the administration of justice can be dealt with immediately, by way of either fine or imprisonment. This applies in both civil and criminal proceedings and is sometimes called a "residual jurisdiction". One of the distinguishing features of this power is the way in which contempt cases are dealt with by the courts, enabling a judge to deal with contemptuous behaviour immediately and as a matter of urgency. There is no trial or statutory procedure, as there is with a criminal charge, so there are strict guidelines to ensure that a person accused of contempt is dealt with fairly by the court. The power of a judge to deal with contempt *ex proprio motu* was challenged in *Robertson* v *Gough*; *Gough* v *HM Advocate* (2007) on the basis that it denied persons accused of contempt the right to a fair hearing before an independent tribunal, the presumption of innocence, and sufficient time to prepare a defence, all of which were in contravention of Art 6 of the European Convention on Human Rights ("ECHR"). However, the court held that sufficient safeguards were provided and that it was the duty of the presiding judge to decide whether the conduct was contemptuous unless the contempt was directed at him personally.

Although a judge has power to deal with contempt, the Lord Advocate or other interested party may also initiate proceedings for contempt, by way of a petition and complaint to the High Court. Certain types of contempt, for example perjury, are also crimes and can be prosecuted by way of indictment under solemn proceedings and by complaint in summary ones. Appeal against a finding of contempt is by way of petition to the *nobile officium*, unless the accused has been convicted on indictment or summary complaint.

THE PURPOSE OF THE CONTEMPT OF COURT ACT 1981

Contempt as a deterrent

The 1981 Act is primarily used as a protection and deterrence against outside interference. This principle is recognised in Art 10 ECHR. Lord Diplock, in *Attorney-General* v *English* (1983), stated that "The public policy that underlies the strict liability rule in contempt of court is deterrence".

A corollary to this is that contempt law attempts to protect a person accused of a crime or offence by ensuring that he has a fair trial free from outside influences, as provided for under Art 6 ECHR.

Contempt laws can also be used to prevent interference before it arises, for example by way of interdict. Where prejudice may have occurred already, a judge may direct the jury to ignore any media reports that might influence it in coming to a decision as to innocence or guilt. The courts have, however, been reluctant to accept that this neutralising effect can be used as an excuse by the media for publishing prejudicial material. This is because the purpose of the Act is to deter prejudicial material from being published in the first place. The Lord Justice-General stated in *HM Advocate* v *Caledonian Newspapers* (1995):

> "Nor can the publisher pray in aid steps which may be taken afterwards by the court to minimise the risk of prejudice resulting from a publication which would seriously impede or prejudice the proceedings if these steps were not taken ... the purpose of the rule is to make the taking of such steps unnecessary, by deterring publication in the first place of anything which might create the risk of such prejudice."

The 1981 Act is therefore used primarily as a deterrent which can be employed to punish publishers. This is the case even if there is only a risk of prejudice, albeit a substantial one, and even where that prejudice can to all intents and purposes be neutralised by the trial judge's directions to the jury. However, this rigid stance has softened in the wake of the Human Rights Act 1998. A judge's direction to a jury may, for example, be taken into account when this is considered along with other mitigating factors such as the length of time between publication and trial. (See *HM Advocate* v *Scottish Media Newspapers Ltd* (1999).)

Position prior to the Contempt of Court Act 1981

In Scotland, prior to the passing of the 1981 Act there was some uncertainty surrounding the law. Concern had been expressed in the media about the lack of clarity, especially as to when in the judicial process a newspaper or broadcaster could face a charge of contempt of court for prejudicing particular proceedings. This obviously had an inhibiting effect on the Press in its ability to report particular cases involving criminal activity. Clarification was given by the Court of Appeal in *Hall* v *Associated Newspapers* (1978), when it was decided that it was from the time of the arrest of a suspect that the courts are under a duty to protect an accused from potential prejudice and only then might the Press face contempt proceedings.

In England, similar problems had been experienced concerning what was called the "imminence test". This was particularly vague and meant that the media in England (as in Scotland) were not sure exactly when proceedings became *sub iudice* (the point at which liability for contempt arises). Indeed, proceedings could be imminent for a long period of time before trial proceedings actually commenced. There were also problems as to what actually constituted contempt in England and this led to the setting-up of the Phillimore Committee in 1974 which made various recommendations none of which was implemented. Change to the law of contempt regarding media prejudice, both in England and in Scotland, was, however, brought about by the decision of the House of Lords in *Attorney-General* v *Times Newspapers* (1974).

Attorney-General v Times Newspapers

This case concerned an article which was to be published in the *Sunday Times* concerning litigation between Distillers Ltd, a company responsible for the manufacture of a drug called Thalidomide in the late 1950s, and the parents of children who had been affected by the drug. The drug had been used to prevent morning sickness in pregnant women and, it was alleged, resulted in deformities of the foetuses of pregnant women who had used it. The litigation had already lasted a number of years when the *Sunday Times* decided to publish the article. Although it looked at both sides of the argument, the article commented on the fact that many of the children had still not received any compensation and inferred that Distillers had indeed been negligent. The Attorney-General obtained an injunction preventing publication, on the ground that it might prejudice the ongoing proceedings. The injunction was, however, overturned on appeal on the basis that the article concerned an issue of great public interest and that in any event the proceedings were dormant while the parties attempted to negotiated a settlement. The Attorney-General then appealed this decision to the House of Lords which reversed the decision, restoring the injunction. It decided that the article had prejudged the proceedings and this amounted to trial by the media. By way of clarifying what constituted contempt in England, the court set out the "prejudgment test". Under this test, any publication that prejudged court proceedings could be seen as contempt. This test was a very wide one and had serious implications for the media.

Sunday Times v UK

The *Sunday Times* then applied to the European Court of Human Rights, seeking a ruling that the above-mentioned injunction breached Art 10 ECHR (the right to freedom of speech). The question to be decided was whether the injunction was "necessary in a democratic society". The term "necessary" was interpreted as meaning "a pressing social need". The court held that it was legitimate to curtail freedom of speech where this was required to uphold the authority and impartiality of a court.

However, in this case there was no real threat of that happening. The fact that the proceedings had been dormant was seen as being particularly damaging. The court held that the "social need" to give protection to the administration of justice was insufficient to outweigh the right to freedom of speech.

Contempt of Court Act 1981

The 1981 Act was subsequently passed by Parliament to ensure that the law of contempt in respect of prejudicial publications conformed to the ECHR throughout the United Kingdom. Moreover, the Human Rights Act 1998 now means that judges have to ensure that any measures taken against the media in relation to contempt are proportionate to protecting the administration of justice.

The importance of this conformity was given judicial recognition, some might argue somewhat late, in *Cox and Griffiths, Petrs* (1998), where the Lord Justice-General emphasised that not only protection of the administration of justice should be considered but also freedom of speech and that "Parliament had passed the 1981 Act in order to change the law of the United Kingdom and so to bring it into conformity with the interpretation of Article 10 of the European Convention on Human Rights".

The strict liability rule

The 1981 Act makes it quite clear from the outset, under s 1, that the offence of contempt of court is one of strict liability. It defines what it calls the "strict liability rule" as follows:

> "In this Act the strict liability rule means the rule of law whereby conduct may be treated as contempt a of court as tending to interfere with the course of justice in particular legal proceedings regardless of intent to do so."

What is strict liability?

In the vast majority of crimes and offences there are two basic requirements for a successful prosecution. First, it must be shown that the accused had the required intention to commit the offence and, second, that the actions of the accused actually constituted the offence with which the person is charged. The first is called *mens rea* and the second the *actus reus*.

Where strict liability applies, the requirement to prove intention (*mens rea*) is dispensed with, which makes prosecution of these offences less onerous. The use of strict liability is therefore restricted to cases where this can be justified on public policy grounds, a common example being the prosecution of motorists for speeding. Here, the prosecution need prove only that the accused drove the car in excess of the speed limit. The fact that the accused did not realise how fast he was going or did not intend to speed is irrelevant.

Clearly, therefore, to obtain a conviction for contempt, under the 1981 Act, it is not necessary to show that the publisher intended to prejudice particular legal proceedings. Journalists cannot argue that they did not intend to prejudice proceedings or had not realised that what they had published constituted contempt under the Act.

Limitation of the strict liability rule

The scope of the strict liability rule is restricted in its application by the provisions of s 2(1), (2) and (3) of the 1981 Act. Therefore, before a prosecution can be successful, these provisions must be satisfied.

Publications   Section 2(1) restricts the scope of the rule to "publications". Other types or categories of contempt of court, such as disruptive behaviour in court, are excluded. A "publication" is defined as:

> "any speech, writing, programme included in a cable programme service or other communication in whatever form, which is addressed to the public at large or any section of the public".

The term "programme service" has the same meaning as in the Broadcasting Act 1990. The definition encompasses all forms of communication, from the spoken word to Internet communications, written reports in newspapers, and television and radio broadcasts. There is, however, a qualification that the communication must be addressed "to the public or any section of the public". Private communications are thus not affected by the Act.

Communications on the Internet are covered by s 2 of the Contempt of Court Act 1981 and broadcasters and newspapers will be liable for material on their websites if it creates a substantial risk of serious prejudice. There is a particular problem for the media in relation to online archives. Potentially prejudicial material placed on a website long before proceedings are active is not subject to the 1981 Act. However, the material may become so if someone is subsequently arrested, and if the material has not been removed. In *HM Advocate* v *Beggs (No 2)* (2002) there had been a lot of speculation in the media prior to Beggs' arrest concerning his involvement in a murder. References had been made to his sexual behaviour, a previous conviction for assault and another for murder which had been subsequently quashed for the lesser offence of assault. The material had been placed in the online archives of the *Sunday Times* and other newspapers and was still available there when the trial began. Beggs complained that this material constituted a contempt of court. The court held that the material contained on the websites amounted to "publications" in terms of the 1981 Act and that the time of publication was the whole period during which the material was available to the public. However, the online material did not amount to contempt because it was not readily accessible and there was no reason to suppose that the jury would not follow the judge's direction to ignore this type of material.

Substantial risk of serious prejudice   Section 2(2) of the Act states that: "the strict liability rule applies only to a publication which creates a substantial risk that the course of justice in the proceedings in question will be seriously impeded or prejudiced".

This sets out the *actus reus* of contempt of court under the Act. Publications which do not give rise to a substantial risk of serious prejudice or impediment are not affected. The test is an objective one, that is to say it is concerned with what the ordinary reader would consider prejudicial. It is also not concerned with whether actual prejudice to proceedings has resulted. The test is whether a substantial risk of serious prejudice has been created by the publication. Unfortunately, the Act does not set out what actually constitutes a substantial risk of serious prejudice or impediment and the courts must therefore define its meaning.

Two-part test   The test set out in s 2(2) is twofold. First, the publication has to create a substantial risk of prejudice or impediment and, secondly, the prejudice or impediment created must be of a serious nature. Both elements must be present. Sir John Donaldson MR in *Attorney-General* v *News Group Newspapers Ltd* (1987) defined the test as follows:

> "This is a double test. First, there has to be some risk that the proceedings in question will be seriously impeded or prejudiced. Second, there has to be a prospect that, if affected, the effect will be serious. I accept that 'substantial' as a qualification of 'risk' does not have the meaning of 'weighty', but rather means 'not insubstantial' or 'not minimal'."

The Lord Justice-General in *HM Advocate* v *Caledonian Newspapers* (1989) stated:

> "in our opinion, which fortunately coincides with opinions expressed in English cases, there can be no contempt unless there is some risk, greater that a minimal one that the course of justice in the proceedings in question will be seriously impeded or prejudiced. The adverb 'seriously' does not require translation. It must be given its familiar and ordinary meaning".

Thus, a publication that creates a substantial risk of prejudicing a trial would not be liable under the Act if that prejudice was considered to be of a trivial nature. Conversely, a publication that was seriously prejudicial in its content would not be liable if there was not a substantial risk that the trial proceedings might be prejudiced. For example, a newspaper report of the trial of someone accused of supplying drugs and which revealed the accused's previous convictions for similar offences might well create serious prejudice to the trial. If, however, there was little likelihood that any jury member had read or heard the offending report then the risk of prejudice would be minimal and there would be no contempt.

Substantial risk

Assessing substantial risk is not always an easy matter, as there may be a variety of conflicting considerations to be balanced before any conclusion can be reached. Courts therefore have to take look at each case and decide whether, at the time of publication, the risk of prejudice was more than a minimal one. In order to do this, various factors will be taken into account, such as the length of time between publication and the trial, the impact of the publication, and the extent of the circulation of the offending material. The following are some of the factors which can influence the decision of a court.

The "fade factor"

The principle here is that the longer period of time between publication of the offending material and the commencement of proceedings, the less likely it is that members of a jury will remember any prejudicial content. Obviously, the publication of prejudicial material during or very near to a trial greatly heightens the risk of contempt proceedings against the publisher. *In Attorney-General* v *MGN Ltd* (2002) the *Sunday Mirror* published an article containing an interview with the father of a victim of an assault which inferred that the assault had been racially motivated. The judge had made it quite clear during the trial that there was no evidence to suggest such a motive. The jury was considering its verdict at the time of publication and the trial had to be abandoned as a result. A substantial fine was imposed.

There are numerous examples of the "fade factor" coming to the rescue of newspapers and broadcasters. There are, however, no hard and fast rules as to the length of time which will be sufficient to ensure that there is only a minimal risk. In *Attorney-General* v *News Group Newspapers plc* (1988), two articles in a newspaper had made allegations of misconduct against a cricketer who then sued the newspaper for defamation. Another newspaper intended to publish further allegations and the cricketer attempted to prevent publication by way of an injunction on the ground that it would prejudice the defamation trial. The injunction was granted but on appeal the court decided that there was not a substantial risk of prejudicing the defamation proceedings as the period between publication and the trial was expected to last around 10 months. In *HM Advocate* v *Scottish Media Newspapers Ltd* (1999) an actor had appeared on petition in connection with an incident involving threatening a sheriff officer with an axe at the actor's house. The next day, a newspaper published an article which alleged that the actor had a drink problem and that his neighbours had complained about disturbances at his home. It also gave details of the reasons for the sheriff officer visiting the house. The court held that there was not a substantial risk of prejudice, as the trial was unlikely to take place until 9 months after publication. Moreover, the jury would follow the trial judge's instructions to consider only evidence heard in court.

The length of time is a significant factor in assessing substantial risk and may often be crucial. Other factors may, however, be present that can lead to a finding of contempt.

Witness evidence

The provisions of the 1981 Act do not affect only potential prejudice to the decisions of juries. They can also affect the evidence of witnesses. This is particularly important where questions of identification at a trial are at issue. Photographs of an accused published by the media can affect evidence of identification by witnesses who have already seen the photograph.

In *HM Advocate* v *Caledonian Newspapers* (1995) a photograph of an accused, which had been published some 3 months before the trial, gave rise to a substantial risk that the evidence of witnesses to an armed robbery might be affected. On the other hand, the court considered that the risk of the jury being affected by the photograph was not substantial by reason of the lapse of time (and lack of detail in the article).

In *Scottish Daily Record and Sunday Mail Ltd* v *Thomson* (2009) the question was raised as to whether the publishing of a photograph of a celebrity (here, a footballer accused of assault) was an exception to the rule that publication of photographs of an accused, which affected a witness's ability to provide proper identification evidence where this was an issue, amounted to contempt. It was held that there were no categories of person who were automatically to be considered celebrities "attracting instant recognition and recall" without other evidence. Yet the court did not reject the possibility that, rarely, there may exist celebrities so famous that the mere mention of their name would result in instant recognition by the majority of the public.

Notoriety and celebrity

Where the accused is a well-known personality it is more likely that any media coverage will stick in the minds of jury members. In *HM Advocate* v *Scotsman Publications Ltd* (1999) the court considered that the fact that the accused was a well-known MP made it much more likely that allegations of intimidation of witnesses by the MP would remain in the minds of readers and potential jurors. The allegations had been made in an article published by the *Scotsman* newspaper some months before the trial, but this was offset by the fact that the accused was so well known. In contrast, in *HM Advocate* v *Scottish Media Newspapers* (1999) the court considered that the fact that the accused was a well-known actor could be offset by the time delay, together with the neutralising effect of strong directions from the trial judge.

Impact

The residual impact of a newspaper article or broadcast at the time of publication can also be a factor in assessing risk. The more sensational the headline and content, or the more distinctive the event, the more likely it is that the jury will remember them. This may be, as explained above, because the accused is well known, the way in which the publication is worded or presented, or because the event that is being reported made a large impact at the time. In *Attorney-General* v *Morgan* (1998) the *News of the World* published an article concerning its investigation into a conspiracy to distribute counterfeit money. The article appeared the day after two men had been arrested in connection with the conspiracy and it contained the headline "We smash $100m fake cash ring". It then went on to give details of the past criminal career of both men, calling one a "veteran villain" with "a long criminal record for fraud, car crime drug offences and burglary". The court held that although there was a probable 8-month period between publication and the trial, the article "had been designed to make a big impact on the reader, the references to the bad character of the accused were striking feature of the article and ones likely to be remembered by the jury". The newspaper was fined £50,000.

Even though the wording used in a report can give rise to contempt proceedings under the Act, whether the court considers that there has been more than minimal risk of prejudice will also depend on the way in which it interprets the words. In *Cox and Griffiths, Petitioners* (1998), the *Daily Record* published a story referring to the accused as "high risk prisoners" and as being subject to "a massive armed police guard". A policeman was quoted as referring to the accused as "heavy duty guys". The trial judge considered that the article constituted contempt under the 1981 Act. However, on appeal to the *nobile officium* the judges disagreed, considering that an article in a newspaper referring to security precautions would not interfere with a juror's ability to judge the case properly.

General impact

Difficulties can arise where there is a "media frenzy". This raises the question as to whether the provisions of the 1981 Act are sufficient to prevent media prejudice created, not by a particular article, but by the "totality" of the media coverage of particular criminal proceedings.

An example of this phenomenon can be seen in the English case of *Attorney-General* v *MGN* (1997) where the relationship between a famous soap opera actress and her boyfriend resulted in several tabloid newspapers publishing articles which contained references to the previous convictions of the boyfriend who was standing trial for assault. The criminal record of the accused had already been referred to in the Press prior to the proceedings becoming active. The judge at the trial decided to stay the proceedings as a result of media prejudice. An application by the Attorney-General was then made against several newspapers for contempt of court. The court held that although the totality of the Press coverage may have had a prejudicial effect on the trial, no particular article or newspaper could be held to be liable under the 1981 Act. Schiemann LJ stated:

> "A consequence of the need in contempt proceedings, in which respondents face imprisonment or a fine, to be sure and look at each publication separately and the need in trial proceedings to look at risk of prejudice created by the totality of publications can be that it is proper to stay proceedings on the ground of prejudice albeit that no individual is guilty of contempt."

It has been doubted whether a Scottish court would have come to the same decision given the prejudicial nature of some of the reports. A recent case demonstrates the reluctance of courts in Scotland to accept that media coverage, when taken together, may influence a jury where the trial judge gives proper directions. In *Mitchell* v *HM Advocate* (2008), which was an appeal against conviction for murder, one of the grounds of appeal was the decision of the trial judge to refuse a motion to have the trial heard outside Edinburgh. The reason for the defence request was that it considered the media coverage, which had been intense and often sensational, would not allow the accused to receive a fair trial in Edinburgh. The Appeal Court held that the directions of the judge were sufficient to ensure that the accused had received a fair trial.

Circulation

Another factor that is important in assessing the risk of prejudice is circulation. The question here is whether or not it would be likely that a jury member would have heard, seen or read the offending publication. For example, a local newspaper with a small circulation in Campbeltown which published prejudicial material about a trial taking place in Inverness would be unlikely to cause a substantial risk of prejudice to the trial. In *Attorney-General* v *Independent Television News* (1995) the *Northern Echo* newspaper published an article stating that a murder suspect was a convicted IRA terrorist. The court accepted that members of the jury at the trial to be held in the south of England, where the circulation of the newspaper was very low, were not likely to have read the article.

However, low circulation does not automatically mean that there will not be a substantial risk of prejudice. In *HM Advocate* v *Scotsman Publications Ltd* (1999) the fact that the *Scotsman* had a low circulation in the west of Scotland, where the trial of an MP was to be held, was outweighed by the accused's high public profile.

TYPE OF PROCEEDINGS

The 1981 Act is concerned not only with criminal proceedings but also with civil ones. However, the vast majority of cases involving contempt under the 1981 Act are criminal ones involving juries. Most civil cases in Scotland do not have juries and there is therefore much less likelihood of media contempt.

Although appeal proceedings are subject to the 1981 Act, the likelihood of prejudicing such proceedings is remote as they are heard by judges only and no juries are involved. However, in *Re Channel 4 Television Co Ltd* (1988) an injunction was obtained preventing the broadcast of a reconstruction of an appeal against the conviction of the "Birmingham Six". This was mainly on the ground that the public's view of the court's judgment might be affected, rather than any influence on the appeal judges themselves.

EXAMPLES OF SERIOUS PREJUDICE

Imputations of guilt

A report of court proceedings which implies that a person is guilty of the offence with which he is charged can clearly be prejudicial. For example, in *HM Advocate v News Group Newspapers* (1989) the *Daily Express* published sensational details of the shooting of a Yugoslavian émigré, clearly implying the motive and guilt of the accused. The newspaper was fined £30,000. This case also highlighted the fact that scrutiny by lawyers of a story, which in this case was by an English barrister, does not release a newspaper from liability. In *Attorney-General v Unger* (1998), the *Manchester Evening News* reported that a home help, who had been caught on video, taking money from a fridge in a pensioner's kitchen, had confessed to the theft. The judge emphasised that just because a person had confessed to a crime did not necessarily mean that he would plead guilty to it. Although the court decided that the article had prejudged the guilt of the home help, the fact that the time gap between publication and trial was 9 months made the probability of prejudice less than substantial.

Previous convictions

The publication of an accused's previous convictions can have serious consequences as such information is withheld from a jury precisely because it might affect their decision. In *HM Advocate v Caledonian Newspapers Ltd* (1995) an article in the *Daily Record* incorrectly stated that an escaped prisoner had previously been convicted for murder. In that case the newspaper escaped liability on the basis of the length of time between publication and trial.

The character of the accused

Reports which contain allegations against the character of a person involved in legal proceedings can also give rise to contempt proceedings. For example, to allege that an accused is a liar or disreputable in some way may influence the minds of jury members. In *HM Advocate* v *Scottish Media* (1999) a report implying that the accused was having money trouble, drank a lot, and that his neighbours had complained about disturbances at his home were factors in contempt proceedings.

In *Attorney-General* v *Hislop and Pressdram* (1991) serious allegations were made in *Private Eye* against Sonia Sutcliffe, who was the plaintiff in a defamation action against the magazine. The allegations were made shortly before the defamation action was due to commence. *Private Eye* claimed that that she had provided alibis for her husband, the "Yorkshire Ripper", and defrauded the DHSS and that these matters would be raised in the forthcoming trial if she persisted in the action against the magazine. The publishers and editor were fined for contempt, not only for blackening her character, and thereby giving rise to a serious risk of prejudice to the libel action, but also for intentionally attempting to deter her from continuing with it.

Matters heard outwith the jury

Reporting details of court proceedings that are held outwith the hearing of a jury can also be dangerous. This often arises where the admissibility of evidence is to be discussed and the jury is asked to withdraw while this takes place. If the jury then reads or hears about what went on, the whole purpose of withdrawing the jury is defeated. However, the position here is not absolutely clear, as fair and accurate reports are protected by s 4(1) of the Act and it is open to the court to impose a temporary ban on reporting under s 4(2).

Active proceedings

Section 2(3) of and Sch 1 to the 1981 Act deal with the question of when liability for contempt arises and the point at which proceedings come under the protection of the courts.

This limits the application of the strict liability rule to court proceedings which have become active under the provisions of the Act. If the proceedings are not active, there is no risk of prosecution under the Act.

Criminal proceedings

Criminal proceedings become active where:

- a suspect has been arrested without a warrant or a judge or sheriff has granted a warrant to arrest; or

- there has been no arrest but either a warrant to cite the accused to appear or an indictment or other document specifying the charge has been issued.

The section does not cover the detention of a person under the Criminal Procedure (Scotland) Act 1995, although it would be inadvisable to publish anything until the person had been released without arrest.

Criminal proceedings cease to be active when they are concluded:

- by acquittal or sentence: proceedings are therefore still active where there is a guilty verdict right up until the judge passes sentence (which can be some weeks later). However, the likelihood of prejudice at this stage must be very low; or
- by any other verdict, finding, order or decision which puts an end to the proceedings, for example where a judge rules that there is no case to answer; or
- where they are discontinued or by operation of law: it was established in *Express Newspapers plc, Petitioner* (1999) that where the prosecution deserts *pro loco et tempore* (in time and place, or temporarily) proceedings remain active, as the prosecution has the discretion to re-indict the accused or serve a fresh complaint. Where the desertion is *simpliciter* there is no such discretion and proceedings are brought to end on the granting of the motion and cannot be recommenced; or
- if the accused is found to be insane.

Civil proceedings

Civil cases become active from the time arrangements for a hearing have been made or, where no such arrangements have been made, from the time the hearing begins. They remain active until they are disposed of, discontinued or withdrawn. In Scotland this means that in an ordinary action, that is to say actions worth over £5,000, proceedings become active from the time a judge closes the record (no further adjustment to the pleadings are allowed) and fixes a hearing. In the case of summary and small claims actions, where there are no written pleadings as such, proceedings are active when a date for a hearing is fixed.

Appeals

Appellate proceedings become active from the time they are commenced. Commencement of appellate proceedings occurs:

- where an application for leave to appeal or review is made or by notice of such application; or
- by notice of appeal or of application for review; or
- by other originating process.

They cease to be active when they are disposed of or abandoned. Where authority is granted to bring a new prosecution, proceedings are active from the conclusion of the appellate proceedings.

DEFENCES

Most contempt proceedings are defended on the question of substantial risk of serious prejudice. However, the 1981 Act also provides statutory defences under ss 3, 4 and 5, although in practice they are not often used.

Innocent publication

Section 3(1) of the 1981 Act sets out the defence of innocent publication. A publisher is not guilty of contempt under the strict liability rule if, at the time of publication (having taken all reasonable care), the publisher did not know and had no reason to believe that the relevant proceedings were active. The same applies to distributors under s 3(2) of the Act.

The important consideration here is whether or not reasonable care has been taken to ascertain whether proceedings were active. The burden is on the publisher or distributor to show this. Reliance on the police or prosecuting authority to advise a publisher is, of course, no defence and one's own enquiries must be made.

There are no Scottish examples of innocent publication. In the unreported English case of *Re Duffy; Attorney-General v News Group Newspapers Ltd (Arlidge, Eady & Smith on Contempt* (2nd edn, 2002), p 257), an experienced reporter investigated a criminal conspiracy to cultivate "skunk" cannabis. The reporter had advised the police of the investigation and agreed that he would give them details of the conspiracy just prior to publication, including the name of the ringleader, a man called Duffy. When he handed over the information the police did not tell him that they had already arrested Duffy. He was told only that Duffy was known to the police. The article, which was of a fairly sensational nature, was published and resulted in contempt proceedings being brought against the journalist and newspaper. It was accepted by the court that, in the particular circumstances of the case, the defence of innocent publication applied and that the journalist was entitled to assume that the proceedings were not active.

Discussion of public affairs

Section 5 of the 1981 Act allows the media to comment on and debate matters of public interest even although this may have a prejudicial effect on particular proceedings that are ongoing at the time of publication.

The section states that:

"a publication made as or as part of a discussion in good faith of public affairs or other matters of general public interest is not to be treated as a contempt of court under the strict liability rule if the risk of impediment or prejudice to particular legal proceedings is merely incidental to the discussion".

For the defence to apply:

- there must be a discussion of a matter of public interest or matter of general public interest;
- the discussion must be in good faith;
- the prejudice must be incidental to the discussion.

As with the innocent publication defence, there are no Scottish examples of the defence but there are several from England.

The case of *Attorney-General* v *English* (1983) was one of the first cases to be decided in England in relation to s 5 of the Act. It concerned an article in the *Daily Mail* written in support of a "Pro-Life" candidate who was standing in a by-election. The candidate had herself been a victim of the drug Thalidomide and the journalist, Malcolm Muggeridge, strongly criticised the practice of allowing babies with disabilities to die or starve to death. He referred to the candidate in the following terms:

"To-day the chances of such a baby surviving would be very small indeed. Someone would surely recommend letting her die of starvation, or otherwise disposing of her."

At the same time as the article was published, a doctor was standing trial for the murder of a Down's Syndrome baby by prescribing a drug that resulted in death by starvation. Contempt proceedings were brought against the newspaper and the court decided that the article had given rise to a substantial risk of prejudicing the trial of the doctor. The case was eventually appealed to the House of Lords which held that s 5 of the 1981 Act applied. The court found that the article had been written in good faith and that any discussion need not be confined to the abstract but could include concrete examples and accusations. The test was whether the risk of prejudice was an incidental consequence of expounding the main theme.

One of the most important points to note in the above case was that there were no direct references to the trial of the doctor. Any such references will usually prevent the application of the s 5 defence. An example of this can be seen in another case which concerned the trial of the doctor accused of the murdering the Down's Syndrome baby. An article written in the *Sunday Express* about the trial implied that the doctor was guilty. In this instance, there was no question of s 5 applying, even if the question of how society deals with such cases is a matter of public interest and concern.

In *Attorney-General* v *Times Newspapers* (1983), a man called Fagan had broken into Buckingham Palace and had been charged with burglary. An article in the *Sunday Mail* suggested that he had had a homosexual relationship with a member of the Queen's bodyguard and described him as being a "rootless neurotic with no visible means of support". Although the court was of the opinion that this gave rise to a substantial risk of serious prejudice, it held that the s 5 defence applied as this was part of a discussion relating to palace security and the Queen's safety which was a matter of general public interest.

Generally, the closer that the subject-matter of the publication relates to a particular trial, the more likely it is that s 5 will not apply. In *Attorney-General* v *TVS Television Ltd* (1987), a television programme entitled "The New Rachmans" was broadcast. This was a reference to a notorious London landlord who had been exposed in the 1960s for the strong-arm tactics and illegal methods he had employed against his tenants. The programme concerned similar accusations against certain landlords in Reading, alleging that they were defrauding the DHSS and harassing their tenants. The programme had also been previewed in a newspaper, under the headline "Reading's New Wave of Harassment ...". The broadcast coincided with the trial of a Reading landlord facing a charge of conspiracy to defraud the DHSS. It included photographs of the defendant, whose face had been blacked out, but he was still recognisable. The trial had to be aborted. It was accepted that the programme had resulted in a substantial risk of prejudice. However, it was argued that it had dealt with wider issues of genuine public interest such as the shortage of rented accommodation in the south of England resulting from government policy. The defence failed on the ground that the prejudice had not been incidental to the discussion.

Fair and accurate reporting of legal proceedings

Under s 4(1) of the 1981 Act there will be no contempt where a report of legal proceedings held in public is:

(1) fair and accurate;

(2) published contemporaneously; and

(3) made in good faith.

Where a report of legal proceedings is inaccurate then it can amount to contempt under the Act. For example, this might include publishing an inaccurate report of someone's evidence in a trial or incorrectly stating that an accused has admitted something which would be prejudicial to his case. Where the inaccuracy is minor there will be usually no question of a substantial risk of serious prejudice. A judge's direction may be sufficient to ensure that a jury is aware of the inaccuracy.

Fairness is more difficult to assess. A report requires to be balanced and statements made in court that are allegations should be stated as such and not fact. Moreover, the reporting of denials of any allegation should be given equal status to the original reporting of the allegations.

Any report should be contemporaneous, so has to be published the same day, unless the report is in a weekly publication. The report must also be "in good faith" which is a term often used but rarely explained. However, it probably means that there has been no attempt intentionally to prejudice the proceedings or otherwise interfere with the administration of justice.

INTENTIONAL CONTEMPT

Section 6 of the 1981 Act allows for the prosecution of contempts in respect of conduct that is intended to impede or prejudice the administration of justice, and this can arise before proceedings are active. There have been several examples in England of prosecutions of deliberate contempt.

In *Attorney-General* v *News Group Newspapers* (1998). The *Sun* entered into an agreement with the mother of a girl who had accused a doctor of rape, whereby the newspaper would pay for a private prosecution of the doctor in return for which it would be given exclusive rights to the story from the mother. The Director of Public Prosecutions had decided not to prosecute, for lack of evidence. The *Sun* then published two scurrilous front-page stories with the headlines "Rape case Doc: Sun acts" and "Doc groped me says girl". The articles accused the doctor of rape and of other sexual crimes. The *Sun* was prosecuted for intentional contempt, as proceedings were not active at the time of publication. It argued that although the proceedings did not have to be active, they had at least to be pending and imminent. The court held that proceedings did not require to be pending or even imminent. The *Sun* had deliberately intended to prejudice the proceedings against the doctor which would have resulted in extra profits for the newspaper if a conviction had been obtained. This meant, rather worryingly for the Press in England, that if deliberate contempt was proved it did not matter that proceedings were not pending or imminent or that any trial might not take place for many months.

In a subsequent case, *Attorney-General* v *Sport Newspapers* (1991), it was held that the decision in *Attorney-General* v *News Group Newspapers* had been correct, although one of the judges, Mr Justice Hodgson, strongly disagreed that common law contempt could be committed where proceedings were not yet in existence. He argued *inter alia* that this would make the position of the Press in England different to that in Scotland. In this case the *Sunday Sport* published an article about a man with a previous conviction for rape who was suspected of being involved with the disappearance of a 15-year-old schoolgirl. The man had also disappeared and the police, who were searching for him, issued a warning to the media not to publish anything about him that might prejudice future legal proceedings against him. A few days, later the *Sunday Sport* published an article revealing lurid details of the man's past conviction for rape. He was later arrested and convicted of the murder of the girl. However, unlike in the previous case, the prosecution could not prove the specific intention required for a finding of common law contempt.

Another example (*Attorney-General* v *Hislop* (1991)) was that of Ian Hislop, the editor of *Private Eye*, who was prosecuted and found guilty of intentional contempt for attempting to pressurise Sonia Sutcliffe, the wife of the "Yorkshire Ripper", from continuing with a libel action against him and the publishers.

It can also be intentional contempt to publish an article that interferes with the subject-matter of legal proceedings by destroying the purpose of those proceedings. In *Attorney-General* v *Times Newspapers Ltd* (1992), injunctions had been granted against the *Guardian* and *Observer* newspapers, preventing them from publishing material from Peter Wright's book *Spycatcher*. The injunction did not, of course, apply to any other newspapers and the *Sunday Times* and other newspapers, having taken legal advice, proceeded to publish extracts from the book. The House of Lords held that this was intentional contempt in that the newspapers had knowingly frustrated a court order and this was therefore a deliberate interference with the administration of justice.

In Scotland, the position with regard to intentional contempt is not particularly clear. In *Hall v Associated Newspapers* (1979) it was held that, under the common law, liability for contempt could arise only from the time that an accused had been arrested. At this stage the courts then undertook the responsibility to ensure that the accused received a fair trial, and that no outside prejudicial influences would be allowed to hinder the court in the administration of justice. Conversely, prior to arrest, any conduct deemed prejudicial to the administration of justice was for the criminal law to deal with. The position was somewhat clarified in *Beggs v HM Advocate* (2001). In this case, prior to proceedings becoming active the Press had published material that had named Beggs as the prime suspect in a murder and revealed his previous conviction for murder which had subsequently been quashed on appeal. It was held that although the 1981 Act provided for deliberate contempt "it would require a clear case to justify the exercise of any residual power outwith the limits laid down by Parliament".

COURT ORDERS PROHIBITING PUBLICATIONS UNDER THE 1981 ACT

Section 4(2) of the 1981 Act allows a court to make an order imposing a temporary ban on publication of proceedings that have been heard in open court. The section states that:

> "in any such proceedings the court may, where it appears to be necessary for avoiding a substantial risk of prejudice to the administration of justice in those proceedings, or in any other proceedings pending or imminent, order that the publication of any report of the proceedings, or any part of the proceedings, be postponed for such period as the court thinks necessary for that purpose".

Orders under s 4(2) are commonly imposed if, for example, evidence given in one trial is likely to affect the outcome of a subsequent trial where they are connected in some way. An application for an order might also be made if the proceedings take place outwith the presence of a jury. Courts will usually lift an order where there is excessive delay for some reason and therefore a ban on reporting would last longer than originally intended.

In *Galbraith v HM Advocate* (2001), an order under s 4(2) was sought to prohibit the reporting of appeal proceedings until they had been decided, or, where a fresh prosecution had been granted, until after the retrial. Although the motion was refused, the media made representations to the court on the lack of any procedures to alert the Press that an order was to be considered or that it had in fact been made. It was argued that it was very important that orders under the section were not made without an opportunity being given to the media to make representations as to why they should not be granted. It was suggested that the court should grant a temporary order to allow time for the media to be represented. The court reserved its judgment on this point and held that there was a system in place through the Scottish Court Service website to alert the media to cases in which s 4(2) orders were in place. It was confirmed in *BBC, Petitioners* (2001) that s 4(2) orders come into effect immediately but become final on the second working day after they are pronounced, unless an interested party, other than the Crown, applies to the court for recall or variation.

Section 11 of the Act provides that:

> "In any case where a court (having power to do so) allows a name or other matter to be withheld from the public in proceedings before the court, the court may give such directions prohibiting the publication of that name or matter in connection with the proceedings as appear to the court to be necessary for the purpose for which it was so withheld."

In contrast to s 4(2), which bans reporting of proceedings or a part of the proceedings for a specific period, an order under s 11 may result in a permanent ban on the disclosure of a name or other matter in connection with the proceedings.

Before a court can make an order under this section it must already have the power to allow the name or other matter to be to be withheld from the public in the proceedings before it. Courts have both common law and statutory powers to clear a court of the public, the most common example being where the victim in a rape trial is giving evidence. An illustration of the type of circumstances in which a court will make such an order can be seen in *HM Advocate* v *Mola* (2007). This concerned the prosecution of a man accused of deliberately infecting a woman with AIDS. The judge made an order under s 11, on the application of the prosecution, prohibiting the media from reporting anything that might reveal the age, employment, ethnic origin or nationality of the woman and another witness, as well as the date of death of the victim's mother. The reason for this was that the woman was in such a mental state of distress that if her identity had become known she might not have been able to give evidence. The judge delivered an opinion to clarify the scope and competency of the order, stating that under the provisions of s 92(3) of the Criminal Procedure (Scotland) Act 1995 a court had the power to exclude the public from the court from the commencement of the leading of evidence in a rape trial or the like. The judge considered that the proceedings before him were covered by this section and that all courts had the power to make an order under s 11 where they also had the power, under s 92(3) of the Criminal Procedure (Scotland) Act 1995, to exclude the public.

JURIES

The deliberations of juries are confidential and any attempt to discover how a jury has reached its decision in a jury trial is contempt under s 8 of the 1981 Act. Even the interviewing of a jury member by a journalist is contempt. The fact that there is no intention to publish is irrelevant. The section states that:

> "it is a contempt of court to obtain, disclose or solicit any particulars of statements made, opinions expressed, arguments advanced or votes cast by members of a jury in the course of their deliberations in any legal proceedings". The section does not apply to any disclosure of any particulars –
>
> (a) in the proceedings in question for the purpose of enabling the jury to arrive at their verdict, or in connection with the delivery of that verdict, or
>
> (b) in evidence in any subsequent proceedings for an offence alleged to have been committed in relation to the jury in the first mentioned proceedings.

In the English case of *Attorney-General* v *Associated Newspapers* (1994) it was claimed by a newspaper that it had not directly interviewed any juror but had obtained the information published in the article from another source who had independently interviewed two jurors in a fraud trial. The House of Lords, dismissing an appeal against a finding of contempt, stated that publication was still disclosure even although there was no direct link between the jurors and the newspaper.

RECORDING COURT PROCEEDINGS

Under s 9 of the 1981 Act it is a contempt of court:

> "(a) to use in court, or bring into court for use, any tape recorder or other instrument for recording sound, except with the leave of the court;

(b) to publish a recording of legal proceedings made by means of any such instrument, or any recording derived directly or indirectly from it, by playing it in the hearing of the public or any section of the public, or to dispose of it or any recording so derived, with a view to such publication;

(c) to use any such recording in contravention of any conditions of leave granted under paragraph (a).

(2) Leave under paragraph (a) of subsection (1) may be granted or refused at the discretion of the court, and if granted may be granted subject to such conditions as the court thinks proper with respect to the use of any recording made pursuant to the leave; and where leave has been granted the court may at the like discretion withdraw or amend it either generally or in relation to any particular part of the proceedings.

(3) Without prejudice to any other power to deal with an act of contempt under paragraph (a) of subsection (1), the court may order the instrument, or any recording made with it, or both, to be forfeited; and any object so forfeited shall (unless the court otherwise determines on application by a person appearing to be the owner) be sold or otherwise disposed of in such manner as the court may direct.

(4) This section does not apply to the making or use of sound recordings for purposes of official transcripts of proceedings."

Photography or filming in court without permission, while not prohibited under the Act, would amount to contempt of court by inter-fering with the administration of justice.

PROTECTION OF SOURCES

Section 10 of the 1981 Act allows the media and others, in court pro-ceedings, to refuse to answer any question or disclose any document that might lead to the identification of the person or persons who supplied the information. The section lays emphasis on the importance of the confidentiality of journalists' sources, as in many cases information is given to a journalist only on the condition that the informant is protected from being identified. This allows the free flow of information and the investigation of wrongdoing which would otherwise render such investigations more difficult, if not impossible, to carry out. The section recognises that it is in the public interest that protection is given and therefore it will be only in exceptional circumstances, where there is an even greater public interest, that a journalist will be required to reveal his source of information. Under s 10, a court cannot require a person to disclose the source of information contained in a publication unless this is necessary:

(1)   in the interests of justice;

(2)   in the interests of national security;

(3)   for the prevention of crime or disorder.

In cases involving s 10 the courts have to balance the right of a journalist to refuse to divulge a source with other public policy considerations which may override that right. The provisions of s 10 have to be considered along with the principles that are set out under Art 10(1) ECHR and the limitation to which that article is subject under Art 10(2). The courts also have to take into account s 12 of the Human Rights Act 1998 which requires courts to take into consideration any public interest there may be in the publication of information before granting any order which restrains the right to freedom of speech under Art 10(1).

Just about all of the cases involving s 10 are English ones and the following are examples of how the courts in England have interpreted this section.

The interests of justice

In *X Ltd* v *Morgan Grampian (Publishers) Ltd* (1991), a journalist was given confidential information about a company called Tetra Ltd which indicated that the company was seeking a loan as a result of financial difficulties. The journalist contacted the company to find out whether the information was correct, as he was preparing to write an article based on the information. Tetra then sought an injunction to prevent publication of the article and thereafter an order for the disclosure of the name of the source on the ground of breach of confidence. The company argued that disclosure was necessary, in the interests of justice, to enable it to discover the source so that it could recover the missing document and prevent other leaks of confidential information. The company obtained the injunction and the journalist was ordered to disclose the name of his informant, which he refused to do. The House of Lords upheld the decision to require disclosure, stating that the interests of justice outweighed the right of the journalist to protect his source. This was because the informant had acted in breach of confidence, there was not any important public interest, and the company might be further damaged unless the employee who had leaked the information was identified. The court also made it clear that a journalist refusing to divulge a source on the basis of conscience, when ordered to do so, was not acceptable in a democratic society.

Despite this decision the journalist still refused to identify the source and applied to the European Court of Human Rights (*Goodwin* v *UK* (1996)). The Court found that the order requiring the disclosure breached Art 10 ECHR and was not necessary in a democratic society. The interests of Tetra in disclosure of the source did not outweigh the public interest in protecting the source of information which would need "an overriding requirement in the public interest". The court also emphasised the need for protecting the role of the Press as a "public watchdog" which could be undermined if this was not available.

However, notwithstanding the European Court of Human Rights' ruling, the decision in the subsequent case of *Camelot plc* v *Centaur Communications* (1998) was that unaudited accounts belonging to Camelot, which had been leaked to the publishers of *Marketing Week*, had to be handed back to allow the identification of the source. The court held that the public interest in enabling Camelot to find out which employee had leaked the confidential information and terminate his employment was greater than the protection of the source.

Conversely, in *John* v *Express Newspapers* (2003), the balance weighed in favour of protecting the source. A draft document containing confidential advice given by a lawyer to Sir Elton John had been deposited in a waste-paper bin and had found its way into the hands of a journalist at the *Daily Express*. An order was obtained, requiring the journalist to reveal source of the information, as there was a suspicion that an employee from a contract cleaner was responsible. The requirement to protect legal professional privilege was held to outweigh the protection of the journalist's privilege. However, on appeal it was held that unless all other ways of discovering the source had failed, a court could not make an order for disclosure of the source. In this case there had been no attempt to conduct any investigation into the breach of security.

However, in *Ashworth Security Hospital* v *MGN* (2002), the House of Lords decided that MGN had to reveal the identity of its source of information concerning the leaked medical records of Ian Brady, the "Moors Murderer", who was a patient at Ashworth Security Hospital. The court held that it was in the interests of justice that the source should be identified and punished, to prevent the same thing happening again. It turned out that the newspaper's source was in fact a freelance journalist named Robin Ackroyd. However, he was not the primary source but an intermediary between the actual source and the *Daily*

Mirror. The hospital, presumably confident of success following the decision in *Ashworth*, then applied to the court for an order requiring Ackroyd to reveal his informant. However, the assplication was turned down. The court decided that the public interest in disclosing the source did not override the interest in protecting the source. The factors taken into account by the judge were, first, that there was a high turnover of staff and it was not possible to say whether the source was still an employee; second, there had been no financial motive; third, there was no evidence of a repetition of the leak; and, lastly, security had been tightened at the hospital and the information disclosed had been neither intimate nor highly sensitive. On these grounds, the judge concluded that there was no pressing social need that the source of the information be revealed. Further, an order for disclosure was not proportionate to the pursuit of the hospital's legitimate aim which was to seek redress against the informant. The Court of Appeal, in *Mersey Care NHS Trust* v *Ackroyd (No 2)* (2008), upheld the decision of the lower court, stating that it had to respect the decision of the judge unless he had erred in principle or reached a conclusion that it was not reasonable to reach. The reasons for the judge's decision had been correct and, with the passing of time and new evidence, the hospital's argument for the disclosure of the source had weakened since the decision in *Ashworth*.

Where there is financial gain involved and the information has been obtained through theft or other criminal activity, or where the source simply wants to create trouble, then it is highly unlikely that a court will protect the disclosure of the source. In *Interbrew SA* v *Financial Times* (2002) it was alleged that a copy of a confidential document about a takeover had been tampered with by inserting false information in it. The document was published and resulted in the creation of a false market in the shares of Interbrew. Interbrew argued that the source was guilty of fraud, breach of confidence, and manipulating the market. The court granted an order for the delivery of the document. The Court of Appeal held that the fact that the source had intended harm by disclosing to the media a document which had been tampered with meant that the interests of justice were served by ordering the delivery of the document. This overrode the public interest in protecting the newspaper's source.

National security

The question of national security arose in *Secretary of State for Defence* v *Guardian Newspapers Ltd* (1985). In this case, the *Guardian* newspaper published extracts from a copy of a memorandum concerning the deployment of cruise missiles at Greenham Common. The document had been leaked from the Ministry of Defence and an order was sought by the Crown for the return of the document, as it was thought that the informant could be identified by markings on it. The court, granting the order, held that it was the fact that the informant might leak other classified information of a more serious nature, and not the contents of the memorandum (which did not disclose any military secrets), that made the return of the memorandum a matter of national security.

Prevention of crime and disorder

There are few cases involving this category. In *Re an Inquiry under the Companies Securities (Insider Dealing) Act 1985* (1988), a financial journalist wrote two articles that implied that he had received information about insider dealing from sources inside the Department of Trade and the Monopolies and Mergers Commission. The journalist was questioned about the sources of his information but refused to identify the informant. The House of Lords decided that s 10 of the 1981 Act, although not directly applicable, did represent parliamentary policy and therefore applied to the Financial Services Act 1985. The journalist was therefore required to disclose his source and it was sufficient to show that disclosure enabled the prosecution of an offence already committed or helped to prevent a future crime.

Terrorism Act 2000

Under s 19 of the Terrorism Act 2000, as amended by the Control of Terrorism Act 2008, a person will committ an offence if he does not disclose to a constable information relating to terrorist offences under the Act. The procurator fiscal can apply for a warrant for the purposes of a terrorist investigation, requiring a person to produce within a certain period material he has in his possession relating to the investigation

Essential Facts

What is contempt?

- Contempt law provides protection for courts to enable them to carry out their functions in the administration of justice. It can be used to deter interference with the administration of justice, to neutralise its effect, or to prevent it from arising in the first place.

- Judges have residual summary powers to deal immediately with conduct that interferes with administration of justice.
- There are various categories of contempt, for example failing to carry out an court order in court, disruptive behaviour in court as well as prejudicial publications

Contempt of Court Act 1981

- The Act came about as a result of the decision of the European Court of Human Rights in *Sunday Times* v *UK* (1979). The court ruled that the decision in *Attorney-General* v *Times Newspapers* (1974), not to lift an injunction preventing publication of an article about litigation involving victims of the drug Thalidomide, had breached Art 10 of the ECHR.

Sections 1 and 2(1)

- Section 1 of the Act sets out the strict liability rule whereby prejudicial conduct will be treated as contempt regardless of intention. This means that in contempt proceedings under the Act there is no requirement to show intention to prejudice a case.
- Section 2(1) restricts application of the Act to publications (including radio and television broadcasts) addressed to the public or a section of the public.

Section 2(2)

- Section 2(2) states that only publications that give rise to a substantial risk of serious prejudice or impediment to particular proceedings will amount to contempt.
- The test set out in s 2(2) is twofold. First, the publication has to create a substantial risk of prejudice or impediment and, secondly, the prejudice or impediment created must be of a serious nature.
- In interpreting "substantial risk of serious prejudice" the court takes various factors into account, such as the publication's impact, its circulation, the notoriety or celebrity status of the accused, and its effect on witnesses (especially in relation to photographs).
- Examples of what amounts to serious prejudice include revealing previous convictions, implying guilt, and making allegations about the character of the accused.

- When deciding whether a publication is in breach of s 2(2) of the Act the court has to take into account Art 10 of the ECHR.

Section 2(3)

- Liability under the Act can arise only if proceedings are "active" within the meaning of s 2(3). Criminal proceedings are active from the time a person is arrested or a warrant to warrant to arrest has been granted. They cease to be active on acquittal, sentence or any other verdict which brings the proceedings to end. They also cease to be active where they are discontinued or by operation of the law. Civil actions are active from the time an arrangement for a hearing is made or from when they begin. They cease to be active when they are disposed of, discontinued or withdrawn. Appeal proceedings are active from the time they are commenced and cease to be active from when they are disposed of, discontinued or withdrawn.

Defences under the 1981 Act

Innocent publication

- A publisher is not guilty of contempt under the strict liability rule if, at the time of publication (having taken all reasonable care), the publisher did not know and had no reason to believe that the relevant proceedings were active. The same applies to distributors under s 3(2) of the Act.

Discussion of public affairs

- Under s 5 of the Act publications which are part of a discussion in good faith of public affairs or other matters of general public interest will not be liable for contempt under the Act if the risk of prejudice to particular proceedings is merely incidental to the discussion.

Fair and accurate reports of legal proceedings

- Section 4 of the Act protects court reports of proceedings held in public as long as they are fair, accurate, published contemporaneously and in good faith.

Court orders

- A court can make an order under s 4(2) of the Act, postponing publication of a report, where this is necessary to avoid prejudicing other proceedings. It can also make an order under s 11, preventing the identification of a person in proceedings before it, where it already has power to have the name withheld from the public.

Common law

- Section 6 of the Act allows prosecution at common law where conduct is intended to prejudice proceedings. Liability may arise for common law contempt prior to proceedings becoming active.

Protection of sources

- The confidentiality of journalists' sources is protected by s 10 of the 1981 Act. Under this section a court cannot require a person to disclose the source of information contained in a publication unless this is necessary in the interests of justice, or national security or for the prevention of crime or disorder.

4 DEFAMATION

INTRODUCTION

Defamation is concerned with the communication of ideas or statements which lower a person's character, honour or reputation in the eyes of other ordinary reasonable and right-minded persons. It poses a particular problem for the media involved in the reporting of and commenting on people and events both past and present. This almost inevitably results in a conflict between freedom of speech and the right of a person to protect his reputation.

Three factors in defamation cause problems for the media. First, the costs of defending an action and the damages payable if unsuccessful in that defence can be high. Secondly, responsibility for a defamatory statement extends not only to the author, but also to the editor, the publisher and anyone else involved in the dissemination of it. However, the Defamation Act 1996 has relaxed the application of this rule to some extent. Thirdly, two presumptions are made by the court, from the defamatory nature of the statement. The first is that a defamatory statement is untrue and the burden of proving it to be true rests with the person defending the action. The media therefore have the onus of proving the truth of a statement. The second presumption is that the statement was made maliciously, and this cannot usually be rebutted. A newspaper article or television broadcast can therefore unintentionally defame a person by making a simple mistake, and liability will still arise.

THE HUMAN RIGHTS ACT 1998

Following the implementation of the Human Rights Act 1998, courts must now take Art 10 ECHR into account. Article 10 guarantees the right to freedom of speech but this right is qualified by various restrictions, one of which is the protection of the reputation or rights of others. Therefore, the media's right to freedom of speech is limited by a person's right to sue for injury to his reputation.

Article 10's influence on courts is an important one and this can be seen particularly in relation to the extension of qualified privilege to media reports which are of public interest. This extra protection came about as a result of the decision in *Reynolds* v *Times Newspapers* (2001), in which Lord Nicholls stated:

> "Exceptions to freedom of speech must be justified as being necessary in a democracy. In other words, freedom of expression is the rule and regulation of speech is the exception requiring justification. The existence and width of any exception can only be satisfied if it is underpinned by a pressing social need. These are fundamental principles governing the balance to be struck between freedom of expression and defamation."

As well as giving consideration to Art 10, a court must also take into account the provisions of s 12 of the Human Rights Act 1998. This requires a court to consider the effect a decision to grant a particular relief or remedy will have on the ECHR right to freedom of speech. This has particular relevance to interdicts and interim interdicts. If the person against whom the application is made is not present or represented then no relief can be granted unless:

(a) that the applicant has taken all practicable steps to notify the respondent; or

(b) there are compelling reasons why the respondent should not be notified.

Under s 12(3), a court cannot grant relief unless it is satisfied that the applicant is likely to establish that publication should not be allowed. Furthermore, s 12(4) states that, where the proceedings relate to journalistic, literary or artistic material a court must also take into account:

(a) the extent to which:

   (i) the material has, or is about to, become available to the public; or

   (ii) [the fact that] it is, or would be, in the public interest for the material to be published;

(b) any relevant privacy code.

The effect of s 12 can be seen in the way in which courts now have to approach a decision as to whether to grant an interim interdict. A person wishing to prevent publication of a newspaper article, or the broadcast of a television programme, on the ground that it is defamatory, can apply to a court for an interdict and an interim order to prevent publication. The court has to decide whether the petitioner has a prima facie case and whether, on the balance of convenience, the interim interdict should thus be granted. In *Dickson Minto, WS* v *Bonnier Media* (2001) the petitioners sought an interim interdict preventing a newspaper story which implied that one of the partners of the firm of solicitors had acted in a conflict of interest situation. The judge held that that, in terms of s 12 of the Human Rights Act 1998, the court would have to be satisfied *inter alia* that on the final determination of the case the petitioners were likely to succeed in obtaining an interdict. In this case, the judge decided that success was unlikely and thus refused to grant the motion.

WHAT IS DEFAMATION?

Defamation is a delict and therefore forms part of the civil law. Actions for defamation are pursued through the civil courts and damages can be awarded not only for injury to the reputation but also for the insulting nature of the communication. In Scotland, no distinction is made between statements that are spoken and those that are in a permanent form. However, in England the former is termed "slander" and the latter "libel". It is still possible to be prosecuted for criminal libel in England, although such prosecutions have now virtually disappeared.

"Defamation" is defined in the *Stair Memorial Encyclopaedia* (vol 15, para 470) as: "the making of a statement or communication of an idea concerning the pursuer that is both false and defamatory and is made maliciously, to the pursuer's loss, injury or damage".

In order for an action to succeed, the statement must be:

(1) untrue;

(2) communicated and refer to the pursuer;

(3) defamatory; and

(4) made maliciously, to the pursuer's loss, injury or damage.

It is, however, necessary for the injured party to prove only that the statement was defamatory and that it was communicated, as the other two requirements are presumed.

What is a defamatory statement?

Whether a statement is defamatory or not is a question of law and not fact. The test was first set out in *Russell* v *Stubbs* (1913) and is:

> "whether under the circumstances in which the writing was published, reasonable men, to whom the publication was made, would be likely to understand it in a libellous sense".

In England, Lord Atkins in *Sim* v *Stretch* (1913) posed the question "would the words tend to lower the Plaintiff in the estimation of right-thinking members of society generally?".

The test is an objective one and it does not therefore generally matter what the person who made the statement thought the meaning was. What is important is whether an ordinary, reasonable, right-thinking person considers that the statement damaged the reputation of the pursuer.

In order to determine whether or not a statement is defamatory, one of the factors a court has to take into account is whether the communication is capable of bearing the defamatory meaning given to it. The pursuer in an action has to set out precisely the defamatory meaning that he thinks the statement has. The court then has to determine whether an ordinary, reasonable man would agree that the words were capable of bearing the meaning ascribed to them by the pursuer. A statement has to be taken in the context and the circumstances in which it was made. For example, it may not have been meant to be taken seriously or have some other entirely innocent meaning. A common example of this is where the statement was made in fun or as a joke. In *Macleod v Newsquest (Sunday Herald) Ltd* (2007) a newspaper published a humorous article which purported to award a prize for the "prestigious Tartan Bollocks Award, which is given to the Holyrood hack who has made the biggest gaffe of the year". Macleod, who was one of the journalists in the running for the prize, was described as being "justly renowned for his powers of invention". He sued for defamation, claiming that the description made him out to be a disreputable journalist who fabricated what he wrote. The court held that the article had to be looked at as a whole and that an ordinary, reasonable reader would not have understood it as being defamatory, but as a light-hearted piece which was not meant to be taken seriously. The article could not therefore bear the defamatory meaning given to it by Macleod.

Innuendo

Not all defamatory imputations are immediately obvious. Statements which are on the face of it innocuous may have a particular meaning to persons who are familiar with the pursuer or his personal circumstances. In *Morrison v Ritchie* (1902) a notice was published by the *Scotsman* newspaper, announcing the birth of twins to Mr and Mrs Morrison, a couple who had been married for only a month. To anyone who did not know Mrs Morrison there would have been nothing defamatory about the notice. However, people who were acquainted with her knew that she had been married for only a month. She was therefore able successfully to sue the newspaper for defamation. Again, in *Tolley v J S Fry and Sons Ltd* (1930) an amateur golfer was shown in an advertisement for Fry's chocolate. To most people there would be nothing significant in this. However, to persons familiar with golf this would indicate that although he was an amateur he would have received payment to advertise the chocolate, which would have been in breach of his amateur status.

Defamation may also arise where there is innuendo relating to the type of occupation a person has. In *Fairbairn* v *SNP* (1980) the allegation was that Fairbairn, who was an MP, did not pick up his mail. Such a statement would not usually be defamatory but because of the nature of his occupation the inference was that he was not carrying out his duties as an MP in a proper manner.

It is not always the case that a statement will have a special defamatory meaning to particular people. It may simply be that the context and circumstances in which the statement is made make it defamatory. For example, the meaning of a statement may be intended to be the opposite of what has actually been said. This can be inferred from the manner and circumstances in which it is said.

Types of defamatory statement

Certain types of statement have historically been seen as being defamatory. However, it has to be remembered that what was viewed as defamatory in years gone by may change with the passing of time, particularly in relation to moral behaviour. The following are some of the types of statement that courts have held to be defamatory.

Allegations that a person is guilty of a criminal offence, a crime or criminal behaviour

Allegations of criminal behaviour can be actionable. In *Neville* v *C & A Modes* (1945) a woman was accused of stealing a dress from the defenders' shop and successfully sued for defamation. Again, in *Sutherland* v *BT plc* (1989) an employee sued on an allegation that his employers had sacked him for fraud and theft, and in *Gecas* v *Scottish Television plc* (1991) a television company was sued for allegations that Gecas had been involved in war crimes in Lithuania during the Second World War. The criminal behaviour referred to must be of a serious nature, usually involving violence or dishonesty. For instance, to accuse a person of parking in a restricted area, although that is an offence, would not be seen as harming the person's reputation.

Allegations that a person has acted in an immoral way, especially sexual impropriety

Allegations of immoral conduct are one of the more common grounds for defamation actions.

In *Winter* v *News Scotland Ltd* (1991), the *Sun* newspaper alleged that a female prison warden had had an affair with a prisoner: the pursuer was awarded £55,000. In the previously mentioned case of *Morrison* v *Ritchie* the innuendo was that the pursuer had had sex before marriage, although it is highly unlikely that such an allegation would be viewed today as being defamatory. In *Finburgh* v *Moss Empires Ltd* (1908) a man and his wife visited a theatre and the woman was asked to leave by the theatre manager who was under the mistaken belief that she was a prostitute. Jeffrey Archer successfully sued over allegations that he had paid a prostitute to leave the country. More recently, Tommy Sheridan was successful in his action against the *News of the World* over defamatory allegations of sexual impropriety. Allegations of homosexuality were formerly actionable, although it is extremely doubtful whether this would now be the case. Liberace, the American entertainer, sued a newspaper in the 1950s, claiming that statements made in an article about him suggested that he was a homosexual. The article stated he was a "deadly winking, sniggering, chromium-plated, scent-impregnated, luminous, quivering, giggling, fruit-flavoured, mincing, ice-covered heap of mother love". However, when Jason Donovan sued successfully, the action was based on the fact that he had been dishonest and not on the inference of his being homosexual.

Allegations concerning moral behaviour need not necessarily concern sexual misbehaviour. They may simply allege that the person is in some way disreputable or dishonest or has acted in a way that is immoral. In *Gillick* v *BBC* (1996) the plaintiff alleged that a television interviewer had implied that she was morally responsible for the deaths of two teenage girls as a result of her fight to prevent GPs from offering contraceptives to girls under the age of 16.

Allegations about conduct of one's profession, trade or occupation

It is defamatory falsely to accuse a person of being unfit for their profession, trade or occupation. For example, to accuse a doctor or a lawyer of negligence can be defamatory. The statement need not, however, allege incompetence but may, alternatively, reflect on the way a person carries out a particular office or duty. In *Fraser* v *Mirza* (1993), a police officer was accused of arresting a person not because there was a reasonable suspicion that the accused had committed an offence but on the ground of racism. In *Winter* v *News Scotland Ltd* (1991) a female prison warden was accused of having an affair with a prisoner. In both these cases there was no imputation that the defender was generally incompetent at his or her job.

False allegations resulting in injury to a person's financial position

In *Russell* v *Stubbs* (1913) the publishers of *Stubbs' Weekly Gazette* published the pursuer's name in a list of persons against whom decree had been granted for non-payment of debt. In fact, the debt had been paid. However, there was an explanatory note in the list, stating that the debts listed could have been paid, and the action was therefore dismissed.

Statements that result in financial loss to a business are also actionable. If a newspaper published an inaccurate story that a manufacturer's goods were unsafe and this resulted in the withdrawal of the goods together with a consequent loss of profit and reputation, the manufacturer would clearly have grounds for proceedings against the newspaper.

COMMUNICATION

As mentioned previously, a requirement in an action for defamation is that the pursuer shows that the defamatory statement or idea has been communicated to him, either by the defender or by some other person. Proof of communication is a question of fact and in the case of the media communication is usually by way of publication of a defamatory article or broadcast of a television or radio programme. The communication must also refer to the pursuer and the person need not be named, as long as he can be identified.

There can be difficulties for the media where more than one person has the same or a similar name. Liability for defamation can therefore arise where a media report either does not sufficiently identify the person to whom a report is directed or makes a mistake in his name. In *Harkness* v *Daily Record* (1924) a William Harkness and his wife had been convicted of murder and a newspaper mistakenly reported the condemned couple as "John Harkness and his wife". This resulted in an action for defamation being raised against the newspaper. In *Newstead* v *London Express Newspapers* (1940) a man called Harold Newstead was convicted of bigamy. He was 30 years old and lived in Camberwell. A newspaper reported these facts and was successfully sued for defamation by another Harold Newstead who also came from Camberwell and was of a similar age.

In Scots law, communication of a defamatory statement can be to the pursuer alone, with no third-party involvement, by virtue of the fact that in Scotland a person can sue for affront as well as injury to public reputation. In *Mackay* v *McCankie* (1883), which concerned a letter making allegations of fraud, the Lord President stated:

> "The defender maintains, not very strongly, that the letter being sent to the pursuer himself and not communicated to any third party, will not found an action for slander. That has, I think, been long ago settled in the law of Scotland. In that respect our law differs from that of England, for our law says that a man may have damages for injury done to his feelings. The law of England repudiates this doctrine."

Defamatory statements can be communicated in any form that conveys a defamatory meaning. Although this is commonly by way of printed or spoken words, the Internet or a television or radio broadcast, "communication" can be by means of pictures, photographs, cartoons or even a statue. In *Monson* v *Tussauds* (1894), for example, Monson, who had been tried for murder, was acquitted on a "not proven" verdict. Madame Tussauds made a wax effigy of him and placed it among those of infamous murderers. Monson sued the museum, arguing that the positioning of the effigy made him out to be a notorious criminal. Although he was successful, the court awarded him only minimal damages.

The Internet

Internet communications can take many forms, including e-mails, the World Wide Web, chat rooms, bulletin boards and other forums. The Internet is now one of the commonest forms of communication and does not recognise any national boundaries. This raises complex problems of private international law because questions arise of which country has jurisdiction to hear an action and which law is to apply. A person who alleges that he has been defamed may be able to choose which jurisdiction would be the most advantageous one in which to bring proceedings. In *Gutnick* v *Dow Jones Inc* (2002) the claimant brought an action against *Barrons' Magazine* which was published in America. However, he sued in Victoria, Australia, for damage to his reputation there. The online edition of the magazine had 555,000 subscribers, of whom only around 1,700 were in Australia. The fact that Internet publishers have greater protection in the US was probably a significant factor in the decision to bring proceedings in Australia.

In the UK, the courts apply different rules depending on whether the defamatory statement was made within the jurisdictions in the European Union or elsewhere in the world. The question of which law the court should apply depends on the "double actionability" rule. This states that a Scottish court can give damages for foreign publications only if the case is actionable here and in the country in which the publication takes place. The same rule applies in England. If a defamatory statement is not published in this country the question of whether or not a court has jurisdiction may also depend on whether the claimant has a particular connection with this country and the number of copies published. In *Berezovsky* v *Michaels* (2000), *Forbes Magazine*, which is published in America, made allegations that a Russian businessman was the head of a mafia-style gang which engaged in murder. The magazine sold only 2,000 copies in England. The claimant had been in England 31 times, to visit his wife and look after various business interests. The House of Lords held that he was entitled to raise the action in England because he had substantial business and family connections there and sufficient copies of the magazine had been purchased.

Internet service providers

Internet service providers (ISPs) face particular problems as providers of access to the Internet for their customers. Where there is no attempt to monitor or interfere with material in any way then the ISP is viewed merely as channel, or what is termed a "conduit", through which information passes. In these circumstances, they are the disseminators, or what are sometimes referred to as "secondary publishers", and will have a defence under s 1 of the Defamation Act 1996 as "the operator of or provider of access to a communications system by means of which the statement is transmitted, or made available, by a person over whom he has no effective control". However, this defence is available to the ISP only if:

(a) it took reasonable care in relation to its publication; and

(b) it did not know, and had no reason to believe, that what it did caused or contributed to the publication of a defamatory statement.

Therefore, if the ISP was aware of the defamatory content, even if it was apparently true, the defence would not be available to it. A good illustration of the application of the defence is *Godfrey* v *Demon Internet* (1999), where an anonymous defamatory posting, which made out that it had come from the claimant, was stored on the defender's news service. The claimant advised the defender that it was a forgery and requested that it be removed. Unfortunately, the defender did not do this and the offending material remained on the site for a further 10 days. The defender argued that it was not the primary publisher and therefore not responsible for the posting. It was accepted by the court that the ISP was not a "publisher" in terms of s 1 of the Defamation Act but that because it had failed to remove the defamatory posting it was liable for the defamatory comments.

The Electronic Commerce (EC Directive) Regulations 2002 also limit the liability of ISPs who host or store information. Article 14 of the Regulations grants immunity on similar conditions to those under s 1 of the Defamation Act, namely that:

(1) it was not aware that the activity was illegal;

(2) once it had knowledge it removed the offending information; and

(3) the third party was not acting under the authority or control of the ISP.

The limited protection given to ISPs in the UK is in sharp contrast to that provided in the United States. There, ISPs are given almost full protection under s 230(c) of the Communications Decency Act 1996.

Online archive materials

Most newspapers have online archives of previous editions available to the public. This type of archive is not immune from liability for defamation. In England, the problem of liability for online archives was highlighted in the case of *Loutchansky* v *Times Newspapers* (2002). In this case, two articles in *The Times* alleged that Louthchansky was a "suspected mafia boss" involved in various illegal activities. He sued and the newspaper claimed that the article was covered by qualified privilege, although the court eventually held that the articles had failed the *Reynolds* test of responsible journalism. Loutchansky then raised a second action against *The Times*, on discovering that the offending edition had been placed in the newspaper's online archive. The action was based on the fact that the archived edition had continued and repeated the defamatory allegations. The newspaper claimed that qualified privilege applied and that it had a duty to publish the articles in the online archive. This argument was rejected by the court, holding that the newspaper should have published a qualification to the online articles to the effect that they were subject to defamation proceedings and could not be relied upon.

A second defence put forward in the second *Loutchansky* case was that liability should arise only from the time of first publication on the Internet and not any subsequent downloads by Internet users. If liability arose every time the article was accessed and the limitation period ran from that time, it would have a "chilling effect" on newspapers. They would thus be potentially liable for online archive material years after the original publication. The defence suggested that the court should follow the "single publication" rule used in the US, ie that only the first publication of an article posted on the Internet should give rise to liability.

If this principle were to be followed then the second action would have commenced after the 1-year limitation period and would therefore be time barred. (In English law a person must commence proceedings within 1 year. In Scotland the period is 3 years from the time the offending material is first brought to the attention of the pursuer.) The Court of Appeal rejected this argument and, while agreeing that online archives did have a social utility, it considered that maintaining them was "a comparatively small aspect of freedom of speech". It also held that damages were "likely to be modest" where defamatory material held on online archives had been published many years previously.

The Times then applied to the ECHR, claiming that its liability for online archive material constituted an unjustifiable and disproportionate restriction of its right to freedom of expression as provided for in Art 10 ECHR. In *Times Newspapers Ltd* v *United Kingdom (Nos 1 and 2)* (Application nos 3002/03 and 23676/03) the court decided there had been no violation of Art 10, as the requirement to publish a qualification to the articles on the online archive did not constitute a disproportionate interference with the right to freedom of expression. As the question of single publication and the "chilling effect" of the rule applicable in the UK did not arise, it was not considered by the court. However, it did note that "proceedings brought against a newspaper after a significant lapse of time may well, in the absence of exceptional circumstances, give rise to a disproportionate interference with press freedom under Article 10".

REPETITION

Newspapers or broadcasters who repeat a defamatory statement are as liable as the author of the statement. This principle was set out by Lord Kyllachy in *Wright & Greig* v *George Outram & Co* (1890). The action concerned statements made in a newspaper report of evidence given in a bankruptcy hearing. Lord Kyllachy stated: "If a newspaper gives circulation to a slander, it is simply in the position of any other person circulating that slander, and the general rule is that a person circulating a slander is answerable equally with the author of the slander."

Although protection is now given to fair and accurate reports of court proceedings under s 14 of the Defamation Act 1996, the rule means that a newspaper or broadcaster may still be sued for simply restating a defamatory statement even although there was no responsibility for making it in the first place. However, the "repetition rule" does not apply in all circumstances and it will depend on the context in which the repetition was made. In *Robertson* v *Newsquest (Sunday Herald) Ltd* (2006) the pursuer sued the *Sunday Herald* for defamation over a statement published on the newspaper's website which had been posted there by an anonymous member of the public. The newspaper settled the action by way of a tender and subsequently was criticised by other newspapers for doing so. The *Sunday Herald* then published an article in the paper's business section, defending its actions. The article showed a photograph of the masthead of the *Scottish Daily Mail* underneath, with the headline: "Lord Robertson launches £200,000 action. NATO chief sues over Dunblane gun lies." The first line of a reproduction of an article from the newspaper stated: "The head of NATO is suing for '£200,000 damages over claims he was responsible for the Dunblane massacre'." The pursuer, Lord Robertson, claimed that the *Sunday Herald* article had repeated the defamatory allegation that he was responsible for the Dunblane massacre and that the first line of the reproduced article in the *Scottish Daily Mail* was particularly damaging. The court held that the article had to be read as a whole rather than looking at a particular sentence in isolation. The "repetition rule" would not apply unless the article could be understood as simply repeating the allegation that the pursuer had been responsible for the massacre. In this case the *Sunday Herald* article was primarily concerned with defending itself against criticisms from other newspapers, explaining the background of the case, and the reasons for settling the action. The article could not in these circumstances be understood as repeating the allegation.

WHO CAN SUE AND BE SUED?

All persons who have legal personality can sue and be sued for defamation. Individuals can sue except where they are members of a class of persons, such as doctors or lawyers or an ethnic group. The reason for this is that a defamatory statement about a class of persons does not identify any particular individuals in that class. If an individual can be identified then that person can sue. Therefore, the smaller or narrower the class of person, the more likely it is that a statement can reasonably be seen as referring to each individual member of it.

Partnerships and corporate bodies can thus sue and be sued for defamation but government bodies such as local authorities and government departments cannot sue on public policy grounds. This was established in *Derbyshire* v *Times Newspapers Ltd* (1993). Lord Keith, giving the leading judgment, remarked:

> "It is of the highest public importance that a democratically elected Governmental body or indeed any Governmental body should be open

to uninhibited public criticism. The threat of a civil action for defamation must inevitably have an inhibition on effect of freedom of speech."

The subsequent ruling in *Goldsmith* v *Bhyrul* (1997) extended the principle to political parties too and the position is presumed to be the same in Scotland.

Defamatory statements about dead people are not actionable. In *Broom* v *Ritchie* (1904), a widow and children of the deceased sued over a defamatory statement concerning the widow's late husband. It was held that there was no right to sue for a defamatory statement about a person after his death. Under s 3 of the Damages (Scotland) Act 1993, however, the executors of a deceased person may continue an action for defamation raised prior to the pursuer dying and which has not been concluded.

DEFENCES

A variety of defences is available to a person defending an action for defamation. Some of them, for example *veritas*, can arise out of the requirements of the action, whereas others, such as absolute privilege, are based on public policy grounds. Defences to defamation actions may be found in statutory provisions as well as under the common law. Statutory ones are mainly concerned with providing a defence which would otherwise not be available under harsher common law rules.

Veritas

As we have already seen, a statement that is defamatory is presumed to be false and it therefore follows that true statements cannot be defamatory. Unlike the presumption of malice, which is usually not rebuttable, the falsity of a statement may be. A defender who can bring evidence to show that, on the balance of probabilities, the statement is true will rebut the presumption and the action will fail, as only false statements can be defamatory. This defence is known as *veritas*. The fact that a statement is harmful or distressing to the pursuer or that other people thought the statement was true is not relevant. This reverse burden has been challenged in the European Court of Human Rights in *Steel and Morris* v *UK* (2005) and *McVicar* v *UK* (2002). In both cases the court held that it was not incompatible with Art 10 ECHR. Proof of only one occurrence of the alleged defamatory behaviour will sometimes be insufficient for the defence of *veritas* to succeed. For example, to call someone a drunk could not be proved by showing that the person was inebriated on one occasion.

Where there are more than one defamatory allegation the common law provided that the defender had to prove all them to be true. Section 5 of the Defamation Act 1952 provides that:

> "In an action for defamation in respect of words containing two or more distinct charges against the pursuer, a defence of *veritas* shall not fail by reason only that the truth of every charge is not proved if the words not proved to be true do not materially injure the pursuer's reputation, having regard to the truth of the remaining charges."

The defence of *veritas* will still therefore be available to a defender even although he cannot prove the truth of every defamatory allegation, provided that those not proved to be true do not materially injure the pursuer's reputation.

Proving truth can be problematic, as well as expensive, for the media. It may be difficult to trace witnesses who are abroad, or information may have been given "off the record" or in confidence. All these factors, including the potential costs and damages, may weigh in favour of settling the action out of court even if the statement is almost certainly true.

Rixa

Statements made in *rixa* are those spoken in anger and are not defamatory where the reasonable person would not understand them as being meant to be taken seriously. No harm is therefore done to the reputation of the pursuer

What is termed "vulgar abuse" is also not considered defamatory, as such terms often have no meaning at all and, in any event, are not usually viewed as having been intended to be taken seriously.

Fair retort

The defence of fair retort allows a person to deny or answer an allegation made against him in a forceful manner and, as long as there is no malicious intention, such a retort will not be defamatory.

Unintentional defamation

One of the harshest rules in the law of defamation is that the requirement of malice is almost always presumed from the defamatory nature of a statement. The fact that a newspaper did not intend to defame someone is not a defence under common law. Unintentional defamation can arise even where an author has created a fictional character or story.

In *Hulton* v *Jones* (1910), a story published in the *Sunday Chronicle* newspaper purported to describe what the Paris correspondent of the paper had witnessed at Dieppe. This involved a made-up character named "Artemus Jones", who was a church warden living in Peckham. The article reported that Artemus Jones had been seen at Dieppe and the offending passage ran: "'Whist! there is Artemus Jones with a woman who is not his wife, who must be, you know – the other thing!' whispers a fair neighbour of mine excitedly into her bosom friend's ear. Really is it not surprising how certain of our fellow-countrymen behave when they come abroad?" There existed a real Artemus Jones (although he had been born Thomas Jones) who was neither a churchwarden nor an inhabitant of Peckham. He was a barrister who successfully sued the *Sunday Chronicle* for defamation, despite the fact that the story had been made up and the newspaper had no knowledge of the actual Artemus Jones.

A similar lack of intention was apparent in the previously mentioned case of *Morrison* v *Ritchie* (1902), where the newspaper had no idea who Mrs Morrison was or that she had been married for only a month. Unintentional defamation can also arise where a newspaper or broadcaster does not sufficiently or correctly identify a person who has the same or a similar name, such as in *Harkness* v *Daily Record* (1924) and *Newstead* v *London Express Newspapers* (1940), referred to above.

Offer to make amends: Defamation Act 1996

A newspaper which unintentionally defames somebody has recourse to s 2 of the Defamation Act 1996 and may make an offer of amends in terms of the section. This can substantially reduce the amount of any damages. The offer may be in relation to the statement generally or in relation to a specific defamatory meaning which has been accepted by the offeror as the correct meaning. This is called a "qualified offer". Under s 2(2) and (4), the offer must be in writing and contain:

(a) a suitable correction of the statement complained of and a sufficient apology to the aggrieved party;

(b) the publication of a correction and an apology in a manner that is reasonable and practical in the circumstances;

(c) payment to the aggrieved party of such compensation, if any, and such costs as may be agreed or determined to be payable.

The fact that the offer is accompanied by specific steps does not affect the fact that the offer still has to contain all the above.

Section 3 deals with the acceptance of an offer to make amends.

Where an offer in terms of s 2 of the Act is accepted by the aggrieved party, then the aggrieved party is not allowed to raise or continue the defamation action against the party offering to make amends. An action may, however, be raised against any other party involved not included in the offer of amends.

Where the parties are agreed as to the specific steps which are to be taken in fulfilment of the offer (in other words, what the actual content of the correction is to be or the amount of compensation) then the aggrieved party can apply to the court for an order to implement the agreement.

Where there has been a general agreement to accept an offer but the parties cannot agree the steps, the party making the offer may take such steps as he thinks appropriate and may in particular:

(a) make the correction or apology by a statement in open court as approved by the court; and

(b) give an undertaking to the court as to the manner of their publication.

The court can also determine the amount of damages, taking into account the suitability of the correction, the sufficiency of the apology and the manner of publication.

Under s 4, failure to accept such an offer by the claimant is a defence to an action of defamation, but the publisher cannot then rely on any other defence. However, an offer of amends is available only where the publisher did not know, or had no reason to believe, that the statement complained of:

(a) referred to the aggrieved party or was likely to be understood as referring to him; and

(b) was both false and defamatory of that party.

Innocent dissemination

Liability for defamation extends to all those responsible for publishing a defamatory statement. This can include not only the journalist, the editor and publishers but also the distributors, wholesaler or Internet providers who may be completely unaware of any defamatory material for which they could be liable. Lack of intention is, as we have seen, no defence. Section 1 of the Defamation Act recognises that distributors may be wholly blameless and therefore provides a defence of innocent distribution. Under s 1 there is a defence to an action for defamation where a person can show:

(1) he was not the author, editor or publisher of the statement complained of;

(2) he took reasonable care in relation to its publication; and

(3) he did not know and had no reason to believe that what he did caused or contributed to the publication of a defamatory statement.

Section 1(2) sets out the meanings of "author", "editor" and "publisher". "Author" means the originator of the statement, but does not include a person who did not intend that his statement be published at all. "Editor" is defined as "a person having editorial or equivalent responsibility for the content of the statement or the decision to publish it". "Publisher" is defined as "a person whose business is issuing material to the public, or a section of the public, who issues material containing the statement in the course of that business".

Section 1(3) sets out the circumstances in which a person will not be considered the author, editor or publisher of a statement, where he is only involved in:

"(a) printing, producing or selling printed material contained in the statement; or

(b) processing or making copies of, distributing, exhibiting or selling a film or sound recording containing the statement;

(c) processing, making copies of, distributing or selling any electronic medium in or on which the statement is recorded providing any equipment, system or service by means of which the statement is retrieved, copied, distributed or made available in electronic form;

(d) as the broadcaster of a live programme containing the statement in the circumstances in which he has no effective control over making the statement;

(e) as the operator of or provider of access to a communications system by means of which the statement is transmitted, or made available, and the operator or provider has no effective control over the operation or provision."

Where the person does not fall within the above categories, the court may have regard to the provisions by way of analogy when deciding whether a person is the author, editor or publisher of a statement.

Under s 1(4), employees or agents of an author, editor or publisher are in the same position as their employer or principal to the extent that they are responsible for the content of the statement or the decision to publish it.

Although s 1 is a useful defence for distributors (such as bookshops) and operators of communications systems (such as Internet service providers), the defence is not available if reasonable care has not been taken in relation to the publication. It also has to be shown that the distributor or other persons protected by the section did not know, and had no reason to believe, that what they caused or contributed to the publication of a defamatory statement. Under s 1(5), the factors a court will take into consideration when deciding whether reasonable care has been taken or whether the distributor knew, or had reason to believe, that what they did caused or contributed to the publication these factors are:

(1) the extent of his responsibility for the content of the statement or the decision to publish it;

(2) the nature and circumstances of the publication; and

(3) the previous conduct or character of the author, editor or publisher.

Thus, if a distributor was shown to have had any knowledge of the defamatory content, or was aware that the publishers were well known for publishing defamatory material, the defence would not apply.

Privilege

Absolute privilege
Statements which are absolutely privileged are fully protected and no action for defamation can be based on them. The principle of absolute privilege is that there are circumstances in which freedom of speech is deemed to be of greater importance than the protection of a person's reputation. The circumstances in which absolute privilege will apply are therefore restricted to particular categories which, on public policy grounds, free a speaker or publisher from liability for defamation.

Parliamentary proceedings and reports
Statements made by members of either the UK Parliament or the Scottish Parliament during parliamentary proceedings have absolute privilege. The Westminster Parliament derives its privilege from Art 9 of the Bill of Rights and the Scottish Parliament from s 42 of the Scotland Act 1998.

Privilege also attaches to parliamentary reports and papers. Unofficial reports such as newspaper or broadcast ones attract qualified privilege where they are fair and accurate. Official reports of parliamentary proceedings and other documents relating to those proceedings are not admissible as evidence in court as they are absolutely privileged. In *Adams* v *Guardian Newspapers* (2003), a suicide letter written by one MP to another did not attract parliamentary privilege as it did not relate to parliamentary proceedings. Under s 13 of the Defamation Act 1996, an MP may waive his right to the protection of parliamentary privilege. Such waiver allows evidence, otherwise inadmissible on the grounds of privilege, to be heard in court.

Other examples of absolute privilege

Judges acting in their judicial role have absolute privilege. Jurors, witnesses giving evidence and lawyers when pleading or examining witnesses have absolute privilege. Absolute privilege is given to statements made by persons who hold a particular office. For example, the Law Officers, the Lord Advocate and the Solicitor-General have absolute privilege in their role as prosecutors of crime. Protection extends to procurators fiscal and their deputes when acting on the authority or instructions of the Lord Advocate. Absolute privilege also attaches to certain types of reports, for example the reports of the Parliamentary Commissioner for Administration and the Commissioner for Local Administration in Scotland.

Court reports

Section 14 of the Defamation Act 1996 gives absolute privilege to fair and accurate reports of legal proceedings in public, published contemporaneously. These provisions are similar to those under s 4(1) of the Contempt of Court Act 1981 which also give protection for contempt to fair and accurate reports of court proceedings. The defence applies to reports of the following proceedings:

> "(a) Any court in the UK ["court" includes any tribunal or body exercising the judicial power of the State].
> (b) The European Court of Justice or any court attached to that court.
> (c) The European Court of Human Rights.
> (d) Any international criminal tribunal, established by the Security Council of the United Nations or by an international agreement to which the United Kingdom is a party."

The report has to be fair and accurate and published contemporaneously in order to be protected. Inaccuracies in a report will result in the loss of privilege. The report also has to be fair and not biased if the report is simply giving the judgment in a case: as long as this is accurate, then the report will be covered by privilege.

Where the proceedings are reported in more detail or on a daily basis then any reply to an allegation must also be reported and given equal prominence. Headlines can cause a problem as they may not actually form part of the report as such. If a headline does not form part of the report then it must be based on correct facts, as it will be classed as comment on the case. Any defence could not then be submitted under s 14 but based on the defence of fair comment.

Under s 14(2), a report or proceedings which, by an order of the court, or as a consequence of any statutory provision, are required to be postponed will be contemporaneous as long as the report is published as soon as is practicable after publication is permitted.

A defender in an action for defamation cannot rely on the defence of privilege for fair and accurate reporting of judicial proceedings if that report contains any reference to evidence which was ruled to be inadmissible in the proceedings because it related to a spent conviction in terms of the Rehabilitation of Offenders Act 1974. However, this does not apply to law reports.

(i) Reporting from court documents

In ordinary civil actions the pleadings of the parties are all written and contained in a document called the "record". Reports taken from this document are not privileged as the evidence has not been heard in open court. There are two stages, the first being where the record is open, and the second where it has been closed. At the open record stage the pleadings are being adjusted and can change from day to day. As a general rule it is therefore very dangerous to publish anything from the open record. Once the record is closed, changes are unlikely although still possible.

Following the decision in *Cunningham* v *Scotsman Publications Ltd* (1987), court documents that are not actually read out but referred to or founded on in open court are also privileged.

Note also that in criminal proceedings no privilege exists in respect of the indictment (the document containing the charges against the accused) until it is read out to the jury.

(ii) Open court

Where proceedings are held in private, any report of those proceedings will not be privileged. For example, in solemn criminal proceedings the judicial examination of an accused takes place in private and therefore reports are not privileged. The media usually publish only the bare details of the hearing, for example "A man appeared on petition at Edinburgh Sheriff Court in connection with the death of James Smith. He made no plea or declaration".

Qualified privilege

Traditional qualified privilege

Qualified privilege, like absolute privilege, is based on public policy grounds. It was defined in *Auld* v *Shairp* (1875) as:

> "The right of a man to express his honest opinion on a matter in regard to which he has a right or a duty or an interest to speak to any other who has a corresponding duty or interest."

In *Reynolds* v *Times Newspapers* (2001), Lord Nicholls described qualified privilege in the following terms:

> "There are occasions when the person to whom a statement is made has a special interest in learning the honestly held views of another person, even if those views are defamatory of someone else and cannot be proved to be true."

The case of *Hayford* v *Forrester-Paton* (1927) is an example of how the principle works. A letter sent by the defender to a committee which had been set up to raise funds for missionary work in Africa contained defamatory allegations against the pursuer who was the missionary. The court held that qualified privilege applied because the defender had a duty to advise the committee about the character of the missionary. Moreover, the committee had a reciprocal and special interest in being made aware of the allegations.

Qualified privilege attaches to the occasion and not the words. It applies where a person has a private or public duty to make a statement and it must be addressed to those who have a duty or interest in hearing or reading the statement. An example of a private duty would be where an employer gives an employee reference to another prospective employer. It is a public duty to report a crime to the police.

The question of whether a statement attracts qualified privilege is a question of law and is therefore one for the court to determine. If a court does decide that a statement was made in circumstances of qualified privilege, it will presume that the communication has not been made maliciously.

The presumption that the statement was not made maliciously means that one of the requirements for a successful action – malice – is lacking. It cannot therefore be defamatory. The consequence for a pursuer is that unless he can show the defender was not discharging a duty in making the statement, by showing malicious intention, then the action will fail at the first hurdle.

Honesty is crucial to a defence of qualified privilege. If it can be shown that the defender did not believe that what he said or wrote was true, then malice can be inferred.

Reynolds privilege

Qualified privilege is an important defence for the media. The decision in *Reynolds* v *Times Newspapers Ltd* (2001) recognised that the media do have a duty to report serious matters of public concern, as long as this is done responsibly. Although, in theory, common law qualified privilege was available to the media, the problem of proving that there was a special duty to publish was extremely difficult to overcome. However, *Reynolds* extended the defence to the media in recognising its role in the reporting of matters of public importance. The decision was strongly influenced by the Human Rights Act 1998 and in this regard Lord Nicholls stated:

> "The common law is to be developed and applied in a manner consistent with article 10 of the EHCR, and the court must take into account relevant decisions of the European Court of Human Rights ... To be justified, any curtailment of freedom of expression must be convincingly established by a compelling countervailing consideration, and the means employed must be proportionate to the end sought to be achieved."

Having rejected various approaches, such as establishing a separate category of qualified privilege (although this form of public interest privilege was later seen as being distinct from the traditional form of qualified privilege), he concluded that "The elasticity of the common law principles enables interference with freedom of speech to be confined to what is necessary in the circumstances of the case". He then set out matters to be taken into account when deciding whether a publication had qualified privilege. These considerations were not exhaustive, and the weight given to them could vary from case to case. They came to be known collectively as "responsible journalism" and are:

(1) The seriousness of the allegation. The more serious the charge, the more the public is misinformed, and the individual harmed, if the allegation is not true

(2) The nature of the information, and the extent to which the subject-matter is a matter of public concern.

(3) The source of the information. Some informants have no direct knowledge of the events. Some have their own axes to grind, or are being paid for their stories.

(4) The steps taken to verify the information.

(5) The status of the information. The allegation may have already been the subject of an investigation which commands respect.

(6) The urgency of the matter. News is often a perishable commodity.

(7) Whether comment was sought from the plaintiff. He may have information others do not possess or have not disclosed. An approach to the plaintiff will not always be necessary.

(8) Whether the article contained the gist of the plaintiff's side of the story.

(9) The tone of the article. A newspaper can raise queries or call for an investigation. It need not adopt allegations as statements of fact.

(10) The circumstances of the publication, including the timing.

Ironically, in *Reynolds*, the newspaper failed to establish that its article about the then Irish Prime Minister Albert Reynolds was protected by qualified privilege. The article, which carried the headline "Why a fib too far proved fatal for the political career of Ireland's peacemaker and Mr. Fixit", alleged that Reynolds had lied to the Irish Parliament. The court held that qualified privilege did not apply because *inter alia* the source of the information, who was a political opponent, was not authoritative, the article had not taken into account a later statement by Reynolds to the Parliament, and it had not given any notice to Reynolds of the serious allegation it was about to publish.

Although the purpose was to give protection for responsible journalism, when reporting on matters of public concern, the standard set by the *Reynolds* case was generally seen as being a high one and the decisions were not always consistent. There was a tendency for some judges in subsequent cases to interpret the "*Reynolds* test" very strictly and in many cases, but not all, newspapers failed the test of responsible journalism having passed the public interest one. Particular emphasis was placed on the steps taken to verify information and to allow the injured party an opportunity to respond to and comment on an allegation. In *Loutchansky* v *Times Newspapers* (2002) *The Times* published an article alleging that Loutchansky was the head of a Russian mafia-style gang and had been involved in money laundering and smuggling nuclear weapons. The newspaper sources of information were other media reports and three unidentified sources, as well as a book on organised crime. The attempt by the newspaper to defend the subsequent action for defamation, by arguing that the article was protected by qualified privilege, failed. The lack of proper verification, unreliable sources and failure to give the claimant a proper opportunity to answer the allegations did not amount, in the opinion of the court, to responsible journalism. This case highlighted the difficulties that the media can face when attempting to produce reliable witnesses to verify a story.

In *Galloway* v *Telegraph Group* (2006), the *Daily Telegraph* also failed the test of responsible journalism over claims that the MP George Galloway had been paid by Saddam Hussein from money that had been diverted from the "Oil for Food" programme. It made other claims of secret payments and demanding more money from the regime. The allegations were based on documents found in Baghdad and the newspaper claimed privilege on the ground that the story was of considerable public interest. The court held *inter alia* that no steps had been taken to verify the documents, as they had no official status, and Galloway had not been given a proper opportunity to answer the allegations in the article or to read the documents to enable him to comment on them in a meaningful way.

Reportage

In *Al-fagih* v *HH Saudi Research & Marketing (UK)* (2001), there was no attempt to verify the defamatory allegations that had been published in an article or to provide an opportunity to comment on them. The difference between this case and the two preceding ones is that the article had not "adopted" the defamatory allegation itself in what is termed "neutral reporting" or "reportage". This type of report is mainly concerned with political disputes between parties and the report simply sets out what has been said by them. It does not imply that what has been said is true or make any attempt to embellish the statements and therefore still retains privilege as long as it is responsible. In *Roberts* v *Gable* (2007), LJ Ward described reportage as:

> "the neutral reporting without adoption or embellishment or subscribing to any belief in its truth of attributed allegations of both sides of a political and possibly some other kind of dispute".

In this case, an article in *Searchlight* reported on a dispute between members of the BNP in which allegations of theft had been made.

There had been no attempt to endorse the allegations or put them to the parties involved for comment. The court held that as the dispute was a matter of public interest and the article had been written responsibly it was therefore covered by *Reynolds* qualified privilege, despite the lack of verification.

Jameel v Wall Street Journal Europe

The decision of the House of Lords in *Jameel v Wall Street Journal Europe* (2006) re-stated how *Reynolds* privilege should be interpreted and has been seen as a breakthrough for the media by allowing them greater freedom to publish important public interest stories.

In this case a newspaper article claimed that the bank accounts of prominent businesses were being monitored by Saudi Arabian authorities for links to terrorism. This had been done at the request of US law enforcement agencies to prevent the accounts from being used for funnelling funds to terrorist organisations. The information for the article had been obtained from "US officials and Saudis familiar with the issues". The article mentioned certain companies and individuals including the claimant's group of companies. The journalist had attempted to contact Jameel for his comment but he was unavailable as he was on a business trip and, instead of waiting until he was available, it was decided to go ahead and publish the article. In a subsequent action brought by Jameel, the newspaper argued that the article was covered by *Reynolds* privilege. The court of first instance and the court in the subsequent appeal thought otherwise, on the basis that newspaper failed to provide sufficient verification of the story and allow a proper response from Jameel.

The main thrust of the House of Lords' decision, in overturning the lower courts' rulings that privilege did not apply to the article, was that *Reynolds* privilege had been interpreted too strictly. Lord Hoffmann, in deciding whether the article in question attracted privilege, divided the application of *Reynolds* into three stages. First, the court had to decide whether the subject-matter of the article was a matter of public interest and, in order to determine this, it had to consider the whole article and not simply the defamatory parts. Secondly, if the article was a matter of public interest, the court had to decide whether the inclusion of the defamatory statement was justifiable and an important part of the story. In doing this, weight had to be given to editorial judgement: "The fact that the judge, with advantage of leisure and hindsight might have made a different editorial decision should not destroy the defence." Thirdly, if the article passed the "public interest test" then the court had to ask whether "the steps taken to gather and publish the information were responsible and fair". In determining this list of matters which should be taken into account, as set out by Lord Nicholls, they were not to be taken as some sort of test, but as indicators or pointers depending on the circumstances of the case. Lord Hoffmann pointed out that: "In the hands of a judge hostile to the spirit of *Reynolds*, they can become ten hurdles at any of which the defence may fail."

The court in *Jameel* was unanimous in deciding that the article was privileged, Baroness Hale stating that "if ever there was a story which met the test, it must be this one".

The importance of the *Jameel* decision can be seen in the subsequent case of *Charman* v *Orion Publishing Group* (2007), which was an appeal against a ruling that passages from a book were not subject to the defence of qualified privilege. Lord Justice Ward, while acknowledging that the trial judge had not had the benefit of the House of Lords' decision in *Jameel*, emphasised that, in the light of that decision, the test of responsible journalism was not meant to be a set of obstacles but had to be decided in the context of the work as a whole, fairness and consideration of the professional judgement of the journalist.

Statutory qualified privilege

Section 15 of the Defamation Act 1996 gives qualified privilege to fair and accurate reports mentioned in Sch 1 to the Act. A distinction is made between reports covered by s 15(1), which are not subject to "explanation or contradiction", and those that are under s 15(2) of the Act.

The following is a brief summary of the provisions of the Act and reference should be made to the relevant section for full details.

- Reports protected under s 15(1) and Sch 1 and therefore not subject to explanation or contradiction are:
  (1) a fair and accurate report of proceedings in public of a legislature anywhere in the world;
  (2) a fair and accurate report of proceedings in public before a court anywhere in the world;
  (3) a fair and accurate report of proceedings in public of a person appointed to hold a public inquiry by a government or legislature anywhere in the world;
  (4) a fair and accurate report of proceedings in public anywhere in the world of an international organisation or an international conference.

- Court notices, copies or extracts from registers, or copies or extracts from publications from legislatures or international organisations.
- Reports covered by s 15(2) of and Sch 1, Pt II to the Act lose protection where the aggrieved party can show that the publisher:

  (a) was requested by him to publish in a suitable manner a reasonable letter or statement by way of explanation or contradiction; and

  (b) refused or neglected to do so.

The term "in a suitable manner" is defined as "in the same manner that is adequate and reasonable in the circumstances".

- The provisions of s 15(2) of and Sch 1, Pt II to the Act protect *inter alia*:

  "(1) A fair and accurate copy of or extract from a notice or other matter issued for the information of the public by or on behalf of –

  (a) a legislature in any member State or the European Parliament;

  (b) the government of any member State, or any authority performing governmental functions in any member State or part of a member State, or the European Commission;

  (c) an international organisation or international conference.

  (2) Fair and accurate reports of the proceedings at any public meeting in the United Kingdom of –

  (a) A local authority or local authority committee;

  (b) A person appointed by a local authority to hold a local inquiry in pursuance of any statutory provision;

  (c) Any other tribunal, board, committee or body constituted by or under, and exercising functions under, any statutory provision.

  (d) General meetings of a UK public company.

  (e) Public meetings held in a member State.

  (3) Fair and accurate reports of the decisions of bodies engaged in the promotion of arts, science, religion, learning, trade, industry and business, games and sports and charities."

Limitation on privilege at elections

Under s 10 of the Defamation Act 1952:

"a defamatory statement published by or on behalf of a candidate in any election to a local government authority to the Scottish Parliament or to the UK Parliament shall not be deemed to be published on a privileged occasion on the ground that it is material to a question in issue in the election, whether or not the person by whom it is published is qualified to vote at the election".

Fair comment

The defence of fair comment is an important one for the media. It allows the media or any other person to criticise or comment on matters of public interest. The freedom of the Press to comment on such matters is one that is accepted as being necessary and desirable in a free society. In *Archer* v *Ritchie & Co* (1891), Lord McLaren stated, in what is now rather old-fashioned terminology:

> "Now the expression of an opinion as to a state of facts truly set forth is not actionable, even when that opinion is couched in vituperative or contumelious language."

There are three requirements for this defence, which are:

   (i)   the statement is a matter of opinion and not a matter of fact;

  (ii)   the comment is based upon facts which are correctly stated; and

 (iii)   the comment is about a matter of public interest.

For the defence of fair comment to succeed, the statement must be comment and not fact, and it is for the court to decide this. Lord Nicholls, in *Reynolds* v *Times Newspapers* (2001), said that:

> "to be within this defence the comment must be recognisable as comment, as distinct from an imputation of fact. The comment must explicitly or implicitly indicate, at least in general terms, what are the facts on which the comment is being made".

In *Adams* v *Guardian Newspapers* (2003), one of the defences to the action was that an article alleging that the pursuer had leaked confidential details of a suicide letter was fair comment. However, the judge could not identify any statements in the offending article that could be construed as expression of opinion as opposed to factual statements.

A factual basis for the comment must exist but it is not always necessary to set out the full facts. To state, for instance, that a picture is badly painted is comment based on the existence of the painting. It may also be that the facts are so well known that they do not have to be fully set out for the reader or listener, who will already know them.

If it is established that the statement is comment and not fact, then the facts on which the comments are based must be true. Comment based on incorrect facts is not covered by the defence and simply to believe that the facts are true is insufficient. The facts themselves must not be mis-stated, as the comment cannot then be a fair one.

Where there is more than one fact, the truth of every one of them does not have to be proved to be correct. Section 6 of the Defamation Act 1952 provides:

> "In an action for libel or slander in respect of words consisting partly of allegations of fact and partly of expression of opinion, a defence of fair comment shall not fail by reason only that the truth of every allegation of fact is not proved if the expression of opinion is fair comment having regard to such of the facts alleged or referred to in the words complained of as are proved."

The comment must also be on a matter of "public interest", which is a term that can be widely interpreted. It can include comment on government, the conduct of public figures, the administration of justice, films, sport, books and other forms of entertainment. It would not, however, cover comment on a person's private life, unless the person has intentionally and voluntarily put himself into the public domain. Finally, the comment has to be a fair one in the sense that it must have been made honestly as well as being relevant to the facts being commented on.

PRESCRIPTION

Section 18A of the Prescription and Limitation Act 1973 provides that an action for defamation must be commenced within 3 years after the date on which the publication or communication first came to the notice of the pursuer. The court has power to extend the period where it is of the opinion that it is equitable to do so.

Essential Facts

What is defamation?

- Defamation is concerned with the communication of defamatory ideas or statements which lower a person's character honour or reputation in the eyes of other ordinary, reasonable and right-minded persons.

- Defamation is a delict and therefore forms part of the civil law. Actions for defamation are pursued through the civil courts and damages can be awarded not only for injury to the reputation but also for the insulting nature of the communication.
- There is no distinction between libel and slander in Scotland.

European Convention on Human Rights

- In defamation actions, courts have to take into consideration Art 10 of the ECHR and also the provisions of s 12 of the Human Rights Act 1998. The influence on courts of Art 10 is important particularly in relation to the extension of qualified privilege to media reports which are in the public interest. Under s 12(4) where the proceedings relate to journalistic, literary or artistic material, the court also has to take into account the extent to which:

 (a) the material has, or is about to, become available to the public; or

 (b) it is, or would be, in the public interest for the material to be published;

 (c) any relevant privacy code.

Requirements and presumptions

- There are four requirements in a defamation action: (1) the statement has to be untrue; (2) it has to be communicated and must refer to the pursuer; (3) the statement has to be defamatory; and (4) it has to have been made maliciously, to the pursuer's injury.
- Two presumptions are made by the court that arise out of the defamatory nature of the statement. The first of these presumptions, – that the statement is untrue – can be rebutted by proving that it is correct. The second presumption – that the defender intended to injure the pursuer's reputation – cannot not usually be rebutted.

What is a defamatory statement?

- A statement will be defamatory where an ordinary, reasonable and right-thinking person considers it damaged the reputation of the pursuer. Types of statement that can be defamatory are:

 – allegations that a person is guilty of a criminal offence or a crime or criminal behaviour;

 – allegations of immoral behaviour;

- allegations against professional competence;
- allegations which result in injury to a person's financial position.

Innuendo

• Words may have a defamatory meaning that is not apparent to an ordinary reader or listener. In such cases the pursuer must set out clearly what meaning he ascribes to the words and the court has to decide whether in the circumstances they are capable of having that meaning.

Communication

• A defamatory statement has to be communicated and this can be in any form that conveys a defamatory meaning. Not only must it be communicated but it must also refer to the pursuer. Difficulties can arise where more than one person has the same name and a newspaper or broadcaster can be liable if a person referred to is not sufficiently identified.

• In Scots law, communication of a defamatory statement can be to the pursuer alone. This is because in Scotland an action can be raised on the grounds of affront and injury to a person's feelings.

The Internet

• The Internet raises particular problems for the media. It is now a common form of communication and it does not recognise any national boundaries. It may be possible for a person to sue in a different country from the one in which the publication originated. Persons who are not resident in the UK may also be able to sue here for foreign publication if they have a close connection with this country and sufficient copies are published here.

• Internet service providers can be held liable for defamatory material. They have a defence under s 1 of the Defamation Act 1996 if (a) they took reasonable care in relation to its publication; and (b) they did not know, and had no reason to believe, that what it did caused or contributed to the publication of a defamatory statement. They also have protection under the Electronic Commerce (EC Directive) Regulations 2002.

- Media online archives can give rise to liability years after material was originally placed there, as publication takes place whenever it is accessed. However, the amount of damages would probably be greatly reduced. Where material is subject to defamation proceedings and is still online either it must be removed or a qualification must be added to the article giving notice of the proceedings and a syatement that the material cannot be relied on.

Who can sue?

- Generally, all persons who have legal personality can sue or be sued for defamation.
- Individuals from a class of persons cannot sue unless the class is a very narrow one in which individuals can be identified. Corporate bodies such as companies can also sue. Governmental bodies and political parties cannot sue for defamation. The executors of a person who has died can continue proceedings that have already commenced.

Repetition

- The common law rule is that a person who repeats or circulates a defamatory statement will be liable for defamation. However, whether there is liability will depend on the circumstances. If the article as a whole can be understood as not simply repeating the allegation, but in some other legitimate context, liability may be avoided.

Defences

Veritas

- Only false statements are defamatory and the court will presume falsity unless the defender can rebut the presumption. If it can be shown that the statement is true then this a complete defence. Under s 5 of the Defamation Act 1952, if there is more than one defamatory allegation it is not necessary to prove them all to be true, as long as those statements not so proved do not materially injure the pursuer's reputation.

Rixa

- This is a defence to spoken statements made in anger, where a reasonable person would not understand the words to have been meant seriously.

Fair retort

- This defence allows a person to defend his reputation by denying or forcefully answering a defamatory charge as long as there is no malicious intention.

Unintentional defamation

- The common law rule that presumes a defamatory statement has been made maliciously means that a statement can be unintentionally defamatory. A newspaper that makes a mistake in a person's name can still be liable even although there would obviously be no intention to defame. There is a defence under s 2 of the Defamation Act 1996 which allows an offer of amends to be made. Under s 4 of the Act if an offer of amends is made in terms of the Act and not accepted then this will be a defence unless the offeror knew or had reason to believe that the statement:

  (a) referred to the aggrieved party or was likely to be understood as referring to him; and

  (b) was both false and defamatory of that party.

Innocent dissemination

- Liability for defamation can arise for circulating a defamatory statement. Under s 1 of the Defamation Act 1996 there is a defence to an action for defamation where it can be shown that a person:

  (a) was not the author, editor or publisher of the statement complained of;

  (b) took reasonable care in relation to its publication; and

  (c) did not know and had no reason to believe that what he did caused or contributed to the publication of a defamatory statement.

- The defence applies to those who have no direct responsibility for publication, such as distributors, printers, Internet service providers, shops and wholesalers.

Absolute privilege

- Where a statement is made in circumstances of absolute privilege it is fully protected from liability for defamation. Absolute privilege is based on the public policy principle that in certain circumstances a person should be free to say what he wishes without the fear of being sued for defamation. The circumstances in which absolute privilege applies are therefore limited.

- Section 14 of the Defamation Act 1996 gives absolute privilege to fair and accurate reports of legal proceedings in public, published contemporaneously. Other examples include statements made by MPs in Parliament, statements made by judges in court and statements made by witnesses and lawyers in court proceedings.

Qualified privilege

- A statement will have qualified privilege where a person has a private or public duty to make the statement. It must be addressed to those who have a duty or interest in hearing or reading the statement.

- Following the decision in *Reynolds* v *Times Newspapers Ltd* (2001) this principle was extended to the reporting of serious matters of public interest. However, not only must the report concern a matter of serious public interest, it also has to have been reported in a responsible way. The court set out various factors such as the seriousness of the allegations, the source of the information and the steps taken to verify the information, which could be taken into account when deciding the question of responsible journalism.

- The House of Lords' decision in *Jameel* v *Wall Street Journal* (2006) re-stated the test in *Reynolds*. It held that the factors set out in that case for responsible journalism were not to be taken as hurdles to be overcome but as indicators to be looked at in the light of all the circumstances of each particular case.

- Statutory qualified privilege under the Defamation Act 1996 is also given to certain types of fair and accurate reports, such as proceedings of legislatures, and the publication of court notices and copies of public registers. The Act also gives qualified privilege to other fair and accurate reports such as local authority meetings, company meetings and the decisions of certain associations. These reports are subject to the qualification that the publisher must publish any statement by way of explanation or contradiction if requested to do so by the aggrieved party.

Fair comment

- Fair comment allows criticism of and comment on matters of public interest.
- The statement has to be comment and not a statement of fact. A comment or opinion is based on facts and in order to have the protection of this defence the facts must be true and correctly stated. Mere belief that the facts are correct is not sufficient. Whether the statement is a comment or fact is a decision made by the court.
- If it is established that the statement is comment based on correct facts, the comment must be on a matter of public interest and must be fair.

Limitation on raising an action

- An action for defamation must be commenced within 3 years after the date on which the publication or communication first came to the notice of the pursuer.

5 OFFICIAL SECRETS ACTS 1911 AND 1989

HISTORICAL BACKGROUND

Official secrets legislation was first enacted in the late 19th century, in the form of the Official Secrets Act 1889. However, it was the rise of imperial Germany in the years prior to the First World War and fears of espionage that resulted in Parliament passing the Official Secrets Act 1911 (the "1911 Act"). The 1911 Act has often been viewed as almost a knee-jerk reaction to perceived threats of German spies endangering state security. Although this was true to a certain extent, s 1 dealt with the question of spying and espionage; s 2 was concerned with the leaking of information from within government and was an extension of previous legislation under the Official Secrets Act 1889.

THE OFFICIAL SECRETS ACT 1911

Section 1

Section 1 of the 1911 Act makes it an arrestable offence to do any of the following "for any purpose prejudicial to the safety or interests of the state":

> "(a) approach, inspect, pass over, be in the neighbourhood of or enter any prohibited place;
>
> (b) Make any sketch, plan, model or note which might be or is intended to be useful to the enemy;
>
> (c) Obtain, collect record or communicate to any person any information that may be of use to the enemy."

A "prohibited place" is defined under s 3 and includes:

> "any work of defence, arsenal, naval or air force establishment or station, factory, dockyard, mine, minefield, camp, ship, or aircraft and any telegraph, telephone wireless or signal station or office used by the state".

Although this section is primarily concerned with espionage, two journalists were prosecuted in 1978 in what came to be known as the "ABC trial" ("Official Secrets and Jury Vetting" [1979] Crim LR 284). It involved three defendants: Duncan Campbell, a freelance journalist; John Berry, a retired soldier; and Crispin Aubrey, a reporter for the magazine *Time Out*. All three were charged under s 2 of the Act for either passing or receiving unauthorised information which had been supplied by Berry in an interview concerning the monitoring of telecommunications by the UK. One of the distinguishing features of this case was that Campbell was charged with collecting and obtaining information that might be of use to an enemy (under s 1 of the Act), and Aubrey with aiding and abetting him. The charges under s 1 were abandoned and the judge referred to them as being "oppressive". All three were convicted under s 2 but the two journalists received conditional discharges and Berry a suspended 6-month sentence. The whole prosecution was generally seen as being misconceived and certainly the use of s 1 of the Act against journalists was viewed as being inappropriate and repressive. The case demonstrates, however, that journalists and the media are not immune from prosecution under s 1 of the 1911 Act.

The police have powers under s 1 of the Official Secrets Act 1939 to require a person to give information if it is believed that an offence under s 1 of the 1911 Act has been committed. They also have powers under s 9 of the 1911 Act where a warrant has been granted to search premises and any person found on the premises, and to take any documents or material as evidence where it is suspected that an offence has been or is about to be committed.

Section 2

This section of the 1911 Act, which became known as the "catch-all section", covered a multitude of offences relating to the disclosure of information from within government. These offences were not restricted to matters of defence or national security but included a whole range of information that arguably could not possibly endanger the security of the nation. Its main aim was to prevent the Press or any other person from receiving a wide spectrum of official information leaked from government departments. The two classes of person covered by the section, and liable to prosecution, were those who supplied official information from within government to unauthorised persons, and those who received the information without official permission, knowing that the disclosure was unauthorised under the Act. The fact that the leaked information was harmless and had no prejudicial effect on defence or state security was irrelevant as long as it was covered by s 2 of the Act.

Generally, Governments and the prosecuting authorities were very reluctant to bring prosecutions under s 2, but a series of high-profile cases in the 1970s and 1980s brought the section into the public domain and led to its eventual demise.

The first of these cases (unreported: see *Robertson & Nicol on Media Law* (4th edn, 2002), pp 556–557) involved the ex-member of Parliament and former Government Minister Jonathan Aitken. He had discovered through a document, leaked to him by an army general, that the Government of the time had misled Parliament by giving incorrect information concerning the amount of aid supplied by the United Kingdom to the Nigerian Government. Nigeria was involved in a civil war against Biafra, a province of Nigeria, which was attempting to obtain independence. Aitken and others involved in the disclosure were prosecuted under s 2 of the 1911 Act after the document was published in the Press. The prosecution case was faced with various difficulties, not least of which were the facts that there were no real security issues involved, the information was available elsewhere, and there were doubts that the information obtained by the general had been unauthorised in the first place. The jury acquitted the defendants and the judge even went so far as to recommend that s 2 of the Act should be "pensioned off". There was a general feeling at the time that the prosecution had been brought as result of political pressure to cover Government embarrassment and that provisions of s 2 had no place in a modern democracy.

This was followed by another controversial case (unreported: see Bailey, Harris & Ormerod, *Civil Liberties: Cases and Materials* (5th edn, 2001), pp 829–830) involving a civil servant named Sarah Tisdall. She worked for the Foreign Office and leaked confidential documents relating the deployment of cruise missiles at an American air base at Greenham Common to the *Guardian* newspaper. She was charged under s 2 and although she felt that she had been morally justified in leaking the information she pled guilty and was sentenced to 6 months' imprisonment. The sentence was generally seen as being too severe and again questions were raised with regard to s 2 of the 1911 Act.

A further case (unreported: see Bailey, Harris & Ormerod, *Civil Liberties: Cases and Materials* (5th edn, 2001), pp 830–831), which also involved a civil servant acting out of conscience, raised doubts in the minds of both the Government and the public generally over the use of s 2 to prosecute persons involved in the leaking or receiving of unauthorised information. Clive Ponting, who worked for the Ministry of Defence, sent a document to the Labour MP Tam Dalyell which showed that information concerning the sinking of a Argentinian warship, the *General Belgrano*, during the Falklands War had been deliberately withheld from Parliament. He was charged with the unauthorised communication of official information under s 2 of the 1911 Act. His defence was that he had disclosed the information to a person to whom he had a duty to do so in the interests of the state (the "public interest defence"). Notwithstanding this, the judge directed the jury to bring in a guilty verdict, finding that the interest of the state was the same as that of the Government. The jury, however, thought differently and acquitted Ponting.

Having failed to achieve a successful prosecution, the Government realised that s 2 of the Act was simply not working as an effective deterrent against the unauthorised leaking of information. This last case may also have been instrumental in the decision not to prosecute Peter Wright under the 1911 Act over allegations he had made in his book *Spycatcher*. Instead, it was decided to use the civil courts and proceed by way of an action for breach of confidence which avoided a criminal jury trial. It is also probable that the ever-increasing difficulties of obtaining a criminal conviction probably influenced the decision not to prosecute an MI5 officer named Cathy Massiter who had revealed details of covert operations against trade unionists and civil rights campaigners, claiming that it was on grounds of conscience and the public interest. However, under the subsequently enacted Official Secrets Act of 1989, any defence on such grounds was to be removed.

THE OFFICIAL SECRETS ACT 1989

The Government reaction to the difficulties of prosecution under s 2 of the 1911 Act was the Official Secrets Act 1989 (the "1989 Act"). This new Act repealed s 2 of the 1911 Act and was heralded as a liberalising piece of legislation.

The 1989 Act narrowed down the categories of classified information and removed any criminal liability for disclosure of much of the information covered by the 1911 Act. The categories of information now protected by the Act are:

1 security and intelligence;
2 defence;
3 international relations;
4 crime and special investigation powers;
5 information obtained in confidence from other states or international organisations.

It also introduced a "damage test" and removed criminal liability for receiving unauthorised information. However, the new Act has been criticised on several counts. The main criticism is that it dispensed with the s 2 "public interest defence" mentioned in the preceding section. Other criticisms include: (1) the imposition in some cases of a burden of proof on the accused to show that the disclosure was not damaging; (2) the lack of any proper defence for members of the security or intelligence services; and (3) the absence of a general defence of prior publication.

Insiders

Sections 1, 2, 3 and 4 of the 1989 Act are directed at members of the security services, Crown servants, such as Ministers, civil servants and members of the armed forces, and government contractors. They are sometimes referred to as "insiders". The 1989 Act makes it an offence for insiders to disclose unauthorised information in any of the categories set out in the previous paragraph.

"Damage test"

Although the "public interest defence" no longer applies, the 1989 Act does provide for a "harm test" or "damage test". This may, of course, involve public interest issues where a court has to assess if the disclosure was in fact damaging. Whether or not a "damage test" applies depends on the category of person and information involved. Under s 1(1), persons who are or have been members of the security and intelligence services are guilty of an offence for the disclosure of any information document or other article relating to security or intelligence. The only defence is that the person charged did not know or have reasonable cause to believe that the information related to security or intelligence or that it had been authorised.

The principle underlying s 1(1) is that a life-long duty of confidentiality is owed by security and intelligence officers. Any concerns they may have about any wrongdoing should therefore be brought to the attention of the appropriate officials or authorities to deal with them under s 7(3)(b) of the Act.

There is also no defence of prior publication, except under s 6(3), which relates to information entrusted in confidence to another state.

Any unauthorised disclosure by present or former members of the security or intelligence services will automatically be deemed to be damaging even though in reality this may not be the case. Officers of the intelligence and security services are thus denied any opportunity publicly to reveal wrongdoing, whether real or imagined, and must face the prospect of imprisonment if they do make any disclosure of information protected by the section. The Government is free to decide what information should be disclosed to the public and what should remain secret.

Offences under s 4(1) and (3), which relate to crime and *inter alia* the disclosure of information obtained by phone tapping and the interception of communications, do not have the benefit of a "damage test".

For all other offences under the Act (with exception of those mentioned) there is a "damage test". The prosecution is required to prove that a disclosure is damaging and that the person making the disclosure would reasonably believe that it was damaging. The test as to what is damaging is set out in the particular section to which it applies.

(1) Under s 1(3) and (4), Crown servants and government contractors do have the benefit of a "damage test" (unlike security and intelligence officers) and the test as to whether the disclosure is damaging is if—

    (a) it causes damage to the work of, or of any part of, the security and intelligence services; or

    (b) it is of information or a document or other article which is such that its unauthorised disclosure would be likely to cause such damage or which falls within a class or description of information, documents or articles the unauthorised disclosure of which would be likely to have that effect.

(2) Under s 2, which relates to defence, the disclosure is harmful if:

    (a) it damages the capability of, or of any part of, the armed forces of the Crown to carry out their tasks or leads to loss of life or injury to members of those forces or serious damage to the equipment or installations of those forces; or

    (b) otherwise than as mentioned in paragraph (a) above, it endangers the interests of the United Kingdom abroad, seriously obstructs the promotion or protection by the United Kingdom of those interests or endangers the safety of British citizens abroad; or

    (c) it is of information or of a document or article which is such that its unauthorised disclosure would be likely to have any of those effects.

(3) Section 3 deals with disclosures by Crown servants or government contractors of:

    (a) any information, document or other article relating to international relations; or

    (b) any confidential information, document or other article which was obtained from a state other than the United

Kingdom or an international organisation, being information or a document or article which is or has been in the person's possession by virtue of his position as a Crown servant or government contractor.

In these circumstances a disclosure is damaging if—

(a) it endangers the interests of the United Kingdom abroad, seriously obstructs the promotion or protection by the United Kingdom of those interests or endangers the safety of British citizens abroad; or

(b) it is of information or of a document or article which is such that its unauthorised disclosure would be likely to have any of those effects.

In the case of the unauthorised disclosure of information or a document or article, the fact that it is confidential, or the nature of its contents, may be sufficient to establish damage

The defence under s 4(4), which concerns disclosures relating to crime, does not, however, have a "damage test". The defence lies in the fact that the accused has to show that he did not know and had no reason to believe that the disclosure would:

(i) result in the commission of an offence;

(ii) facilitate an escape from legal custody or any other act prejudicial to the safekeeping of a person in legal custody; or

(iii) impede the prevention or detection of offences or the apprehension or prosecution of suspected offenders. Disclosure of any of these three categories is otherwise an offence.

Nor are there any "damage tests" for offences under s 4(3) which applies to:

"(a) any information obtained by reason of the interception of any communication in obedience to a warrant issued under section 2 of the Interception of Communications Act 1985, any information relating to the obtaining of information by reason of any such interception and any document or other article which is or has been used or held for use in, or has been obtained by reason of, any such interception; and

(b) any information obtained by reason of action authorised by a warrant issued under section 3 of the Security Service Act 1989, any information relating to the obtaining of information by reason of any such action and any document or other article which is or has been used or held for use in, or has been obtained by reason of, any such action."

Generally, the "damage tests", where applicable, are broad and wide ranging, using such terms as "damaging the capability of the armed forces" and "endangering the interests of the United Kingdom abroad". Whether the latter would include revelations of government involvement in torture or other illegal activities prohibited by international law is, however, unlikely.

There is also a defence, under ss 1(5), 2(3), 3(3) and 4(5), where the accused has to show "that at the time of the alleged offence he did not know, and had no reasonable cause to believe, that the information, document or article in question" related to the category of information protected by the particular section.

Section 7 provides a further statutory defence. Here, liability is avoided where there has been disclosure of protected information which has been authorised in terms of the section (for example, where a Crown servant has an official duty to do so).

THE EUROPEAN CONVENTION ON HUMAN RIGHTS

The question of the compatibility of ss 1 and 4(1) and (3) with the European Convention on Human Rights was decided in *R* v *Shayler* (2002). David Shayler was a former member of MI5 and claimed to have become disillusioned with the way in which the service was being run. He contacted the *Mail on Sunday* which published an article based on information supplied by Shayler. The article gave details of the phone tapping and surveillance of two politicians and a journalist. Following further revelations in the *Mail on Sunday*, also broadcast on the BBC and published in the *Guardian*, of a plot involving MI6 assassinating Colonel Gaddafi, Shayler was charged under ss 1(1) and 4(1) of the 1989 Act. Shayler's defence was that ss 1 and 4 of the Act do not provide a "damage test" or "public interest defence", and were therefore in violation of ECHR. The House of Lords held that the total ban on disclosures did not contravene Art 10 ECHR. The decision was based on the terms of s 7 of the Act, where prior permission for disclosure is provided for if officially authorised.

Lord Hope justified the decision as follows:

> "The crux of this case is whether the safeguards built into the Official Secrets Act 1989 are sufficient to ensure that unlawfulness and irregularity can be reported to those with the power and duty to take effective action, that the power to withhold authorisation to publish is not abused and that proper disclosures are not stifled. In my opinion the procedures discussed above, properly applied, provide sufficient and effective safeguards. It

is, however, necessary that a member or former member of a relevant service should avail himself of the procedures available to him under the Act. A former member of a relevant service, prosecuted for making an unauthorised disclosure, cannot defend himself by contending that if he had made disclosure under section 7(3)(a) no notice or action would have been taken or that if he had sought authorisation under section 7(3)(b) it would have been refused. If a person who has given a binding undertaking of confidentiality seeks to be relieved, even in part, from that undertaking he must seek authorisation and, if so advised, challenge any refusal of authorisation. If that refusal is upheld by the courts, it must, however reluctantly, be accepted. I am satisfied that sections 1(1) and 4(1) and (3) of the OSA 1989 are compatible with article 10 of the convention."

THE REVERSE BURDEN OF PROOF

The second case to raise questions about the compatibility of the 1989 Act with the ECHR was *R* v *Keogh* (2007). David Keogh was a Cabinet Office communications officer who had leaked to his co-defendant, a political researcher, a letter which contained highly sensitive information. The letter contained a record of discussions between the then Prime Minister, Tony Blair, and President of the United States, George Bush, about policy in Iraq and the handover of power to the Iraqi Government. A photocopy of the letter was then put in among the papers of an MP who reported the matter to the police. Keogh was charged under ss 2 and 3 of the 1989 Act, relating to defence and international relations. At a preliminary hearing, Keogh argued that a reverse burden of proof was created in the defences under ss 2(3) and 3 of the 1989 Act, where there is a requirement for the accused to show that there was nothing in the disclosure he knew or should have been aware of that would be damaging. (A reverse burden of proof is where the accused has to prove his innocence rather than the prosecution prove his guilt.) This requirement infringed the right to a presumption of innocence (and was thus not compatible with the right to a fair trial and the presumption of innocence under Art 6 EHCR).

The Court of Appeal decided, rather tortuously, that ss 2(3) and 3(4), when giving them their natural meaning, did require a reverse burden of proof and were indeed incompatible with Art 6. However, it was held that the Act could operate effectively without the imposition of the reverse burden and that the subsections should be "read down" by applying a similar interpretation to that given under s 118 of the

Terrorism Act 2000. The provisions of this Act had also been subject to the problem of a reverse burden of proof.

NECESSITY

The question of necessity was discussed by the Court of Appeal in the aforementioned *Shayler* prosecution, where it was held that it did apply to offences under the 1989 Act. It is available where the steps taken by the accused were a proportionate response to an imminent threat of death or injury to the accused or persons for whom the accused could reasonably be seen as being responsible. The House of Lords agreed, but in *Shayler* the defence was not available as there was no such threat. However, the defence of necessity appears to have been one of the factors in the decision not to proceed with the prosecution of GCHQ employee Katherine Gunn which is discussed in the following section.

PROSECUTIONS UNDER THE 1989 ACT

There have not been many prosecutions under the Official Secrets Act 1989. One of the first involved two men accused of attempting to sell to the Russians a secret acoustic tile used to cover the surfaces of Trident nuclear submarines. The tile had been stolen by one of the men who was a security guard. The motivation in this case appears to have been simple greed and they both pled guilty to offences under s 2 of the Act.

Other cases have attracted criticism or controversy in one way or another.

The *Shayler* and *Keogh* prosecutions highlighted the difficulties associated with the 1989 Act and its relationship with the ECHR, although in both cases there were convictions.

Problems of prosecuting civil servants and security and intelligence officers, where the disclosures are motivated by conscience rather than financial gain, have not really been resolved. The prosecution of David Keogh, for example, was described in the *Independent* of 10 May 2007 as being a "farce" and it was said that the Government had made examples of the two accused "to protect Tony Blair's embarrassment about what he had said to President Bush's Security and Intelligence officers".

The difficulties that Governments face when dealing with disaffected ex-members of the security and intelligence services have also not gone away. For example, in 1997 Richard Tomlinson, who had been involved in an unfair dismissal case following his departure from the security services, was accused of retaining classified material, obtained when he had worked for the security services, for the purposes of publishing a book. He later pled guilty to disclosing confidential information to his publishers and was sentenced to 12 months' imprisonment. After his release, the Government pursued him in New Zealand and Switzerland, obtaining injunctions in both countries against publication of unauthorised information. (For further details, see Bailey, Harris & Omerod, *Civil Liberties Cases and Materials* (5th edn, Butterworths), pp 834–835.)

Problems of prosecution under the Act have also been highlighted by several high-profile cases where the charges against the accused have been withdrawn. In each case, the Government faced criticism for bringing the prosecutions in the first place and there was a strong suspicion among civil liberty campaigners that they had more to do with political embarrassment than national security. For example, in 1998, a journalist, Tony Geraghty, who was an ex-squadron leader in the RAF, was prosecuted after the publication of his book entitled *The Irish War* (*Guardian*, 26 February 2000). The book contained information about computer surveillance by the army and intelligence services in Northern Ireland. Geraghty was then prosecuted under s 5 of the Act but the charges were eventually dropped. There had been no attempt to prevent publication of the book and it was difficult to understand how the information was in any way damaging. Nigel Wylde, who had been a bomb disposal officer in Northern Ireland, was also charged with supplying classified information to Geraghty. This charge was also eventually withdrawn when it became apparent that the information was already well known to the Provisional IRA.

The prosecution of civil servant Katherine Gunn was also abandoned amid speculation that the Government was worried about the disclosure of secret documents during the trial and, in particular, the advice given by the Attorney-General about the legality of the war in Iraq, although this was later denied. Gunn had leaked to the *Observer* a memo which contained a request by the United States to the United Kingdom to tap the telephones of those countries likely to vote against the Iraq war in the United Nations. She was charged under s 1 of the 1989 Act and pled not guilty. The prosecution decided not to offer any case against her.

The abandoning of the Gunn prosecution resulted in the Government announcing that a review of the provisions of the 1989 Act was necessary. However, more recently, in 2008 Derek Pasquill, a Foreign Office civil servant, faced six charges under the 1989 Act (*Guardian*, 10 January 2008). They concerned the leaking of documents to the *Observer* and the *New Statesman*. These contained information relating to the rendition of suspected terrorists by the United States to countries where they could be tortured as well as information on what the UK Government knew about the practice. They also related to government policy towards the Muslim community in the UK. All the charges were withdrawn, apparently on the basis that it would have been very difficult to prove that the leaked documents had caused damage. This was because internal Foreign Office papers admitted that the revelations, far from being damaging, actually encouraged debate on these controversial issues.

OUTSIDERS

Section 5 of the 1989 Act

From the cases discussed in the previous section it can thus be argued that the main beneficiaries of the 1989 Act are the Press and the media who no longer face criminal charges for receiving unauthorised information. Indeed, it appears to be the civil servants or members of the security services who have faced prosecution for passing unauthorised information to them.

In 1999, a Royal Navy petty officer was sentenced to 12 months' imprisonment for leaking information to the *Sun* about the threat of the use of biological weapons by Iraq against the United Kingdom in return for a payment of £10,000. The *Sun* was not prosecuted even though it published the information.

The Press may, of course, be required to reveal the sources of the information, and face government injunctions or interdicts preventing publication of sensitive information or orders requiring the return of leaked documents. Section 5 of the 1989 Act is the most important section as far as the media are concerned.

Under s 5(1) and (2), a journalist, or any other person, is guilty of an offence of disclosing without lawful authority information protected under the Act that has come into his possession where:

(1) a Crown servant has disclosed the information document or other article to him without lawful authority; or

(2) the information, document or other article has been entrusted to him by a Crown servant on terms "requiring it to be held in confidence or in circumstances in which the Crown servant or government contractor could reasonably expect that it would be so held"; or

(3) the information, document or other article was received from someone who received the information in confidence from a Crown servant.

The section therefore covers situations where information is directly but unlawfully leaked to a journalist or it has been entrusted in confidence to him. It also applies where the information has been passed on to him by another person who received the information in confidence.

An example of the use of s 5 can be seen in *Keogh* where the letter leaked by Keogh to a political researcher was then disclosed by him to an MP. The researcher was then prosecuted under the 1989 Act. Similarly, Tony Geraghty was prosecuted under s 5 for disclosing information that he had received in his book.

Here, unlike with Crown servants, there is no problem with having to prove that a disclosure was not damaging. The accused must:

(a) know or have reasonable cause to believe that the information falls within one of the categories protected by ss 1, 2 and 3 (security, defence and international relations);

(b) have disclosed the information, knowing or having reasonable cause to believe that it would be damaging; and

(c) have come into possession of the information in a way prescribed by s 5(1) described above.

Where the information falls within the categories of information protected by ss 1, 2 and 3 of the Act, the test for damage is the same as it is for Crown servants and government contractors.

There is, of course, no "damage test" under s 4(3). Therefore, the disclosure by a journalist of information involving Government phone tapping which has been leaked to him by a member of the security and intelligence services will place both parties in the same position in that neither will have the benefit of a "damage test". However, if the leaked information concerned a security or intelligence matter covered by the Act, the security officer would automatically be guilty of an offence but the prosecution would have to prove that the disclosure was damaging in the case of the journalist.

Journalists and other persons will, however, also commit an offence if they disclose information, a document or other article, knowing or having reasonable cause to believe that it came into their possession as a result of a contravention of s 1 of the 1911 Act, under s 5(6) of the 1989 Act

Generally, a person will not, however, commit an offence where the information disclosed was not received from a British citizen or the disclosure did not take place in the UK.

Section 6 of the Act also affects the media. It makes it an offence to disclose information relating to security, defence or international relations that has been entrusted in confidence by the UK Government to other states or international organisations. The information does not need to have been disclosed by a Crown servant or government contractor and it is not an offence where the disclosure is authorised by the state or organisation or a member of the organisation. The information will be deemed to be confidential if it is communicated "on terms requiring it to be held in confidence or in circumstances in which the person communicating it could reasonably expect that it would be so held". As with s 5, it has to be shown that the accused knew or had reasonable cause to believe that the disclosure would be damaging, the "damage test" being the same as it would be for a Crown servant or government contractor under the relevant section. There is also a "prior publication defence" under s 6(3). Under this section a person will not commit an offence if the information, document or article had previously been made available to the public with the authority of the state or organisation concerned or, in the case of an organisation, a member of that organisation.

DA NOTICES

The DA Notice system (which replaced the D Notice system in 1993) is a voluntary one. Its purpose is to give the Press and broadcasting organisations guidance on matters of national security. The Defence Press and Broadcasting Advisory Committee is responsible for the operation of the system. The Committee consists of the Chairman, who is the Permanent Under Secretary of State at the Ministry of Defence; a Vice-Chairman who represents the media; four government members from the Home Office, the Ministry of Defence, the Foreign and Commonwealth Office and the Cabinet Office; 13 members representing the media, of which nine are from the print media and four from the broadcast media. There is also a full-time Secretary as well as a part-time Deputy Secretary. The Committee meets twice a year. At these meetings a report is presented, reviewing what advice and guidance has been given over the previous 6 months, and consideration is given to updating the notices. There are at present five standing DA Notices:

(1) military operations, plans and capabilities;
(2) nuclear and non-nuclear weapons and equipment;
(3) ciphers and secure communications;
(4) sensitive installations and home addresses;
(5) United Kingdom security and intelligence services and special services.

The Secretary or Deputy-Secretary is available at all times to give advice to the Government and the media but any advice given is not legally binding and is restricted to national security. The question of the legality of this advice was highlighted in the Aitken case, referred to above, where Aitken sought the opinion of the Secretary and was advised that his story about the supply of military aid to the Nigerian Government was not a matter of national security and therefore not covered by any of the D Notices applicable at the time. Aitken apparently understood this to mean that he would be immune from prosecution. He was, however, later charged under s 2 of the 1911 Act. The media have to therefore balance the advice given under the DA Notice system with the requirement to inform the public and considerations of offences under the Official Secrets Acts.

The type of advice sought has been on such diverse matters as the kidnap of UK citizens abroad, counter-terrorism operations and the actions of UK forces in Iraq and Afghanistan. The purpose of the DA Notice system has, to a certain extent, been undermined by the advances in communications. This means that sensitive information can be disseminated immediately over the Internet or by use of mobile phones and digital cameras, and the introduction of Google Earth makes the viewing of secret government installations much easier than it used to be. However, it is still a useful system which brings the Government and the media together to ensure, as far as possible, that sensitive information relating to security is published in a responsible manner.

Essential Facts

Official Secrets Act 1911

- Section 1 of the Act is primarily concerned with espionage. However, two journalists were prosecuted in 1978 in the "ABC trial" under s 1, although the charges were subsequently dropped. They were, however, successfully prosecuted under s 2 of the Act. Section 1 of the Act is still in force

- Section 2 of the 1911 Act was known as the "catch all" section because of the number of offences which related to the disclosure of government information. It gradually fell into disrepute after a series of controversial prosecutions, most of which were unsuccessful. The Government decided that new legislation was required and passed the 1989 Official Secrets Act.

Official Secrets Act 1989

- The 1989 Act narrowed down the categories of information which were classified under s 2 of the 1911 Act. The categories are: Security and intelligence; Defence; International relations; Crime and special investigation powers; Information obtained in confidence from other states or international organisations;

Insiders

- Sections 1, 2, 3 and 4 of the 1989 Act make it an offence for insiders to disclose unauthorised information in any of the categories. Insiders are members of the security services, Crown servants, such as Ministers, civil servants and members of the armed forces and government contractors.

"Damage test"

- The Act dispensed with the "public interest defence" under s 2 of the 1911 Act and replaced it with a "damage test". Disclosures which are not damaging are not covered by the Act. There is no "damage test" for members of the security services for disclosing information relating to security or intelligence. There is also no "damage test" generally for the disclosure of information relating to crime or government phone tapping, interception of letters, or other communications.
- There is a "damage test" for Crown servants and government contractors except where the information relates to government interception of communications.
- The "damage tests" are set out in the Act for each category on information.
- There is also a general defence that an accused did not know and had no reason to believe the information disclosed related to the category of information protected.
- The decision in *R* v *Shayler* (2002) confirmed that the lack of a "damage test" for the disclosure of information by members and former members of the security services was compatible with the ECHR.

Outsiders

- Persons who are not Crown servants, members of the security services or government contractors will commit an offence under s 5 of the

Act by disclosing protected information that has come into their possession where: (a) a Crown servant has disclosed the information or document; (b) the information was entrusted to the person to be held in confidence; or (c) the information or document was received from someone else who had received the information in confidence from a Crown servant.

- Under s 6 of the Act it is an offence for a person to disclose information relating to security, defence or international relations that has been entrusted in confidence by the UK Government to other states or international organisations.

DA Notices

- The DA Notice system is a voluntary one and its purpose is to give guidance to the Press and broadcasters on matters contained in the notices. The media will normally comply with a notice but they are not legally binding. The Defence Press and Broadcasting Advisory Committee is responsible for the running of the system and there is a Secretary who gives advice to the media on matters relating to the notices.

- There are five DA Notices which cover: military operations, plans and capabilities; nuclear and non-nuclear weapons and equipment; ciphers and secure communications; sensitive installations and home addresses; United Kingdom security and intelligence services and special services.

6 RACIAL AND RELIGIOUS HATRED AND OBSCENITY

PUBLIC ORDER ACT 1986

Statutory provisions under the Public Order Act 1986 make it an offence to use or publish statements which incite racial or religious hatred. Part 3 of the 1986 Act deals with the use and publication of statements which incite racial hatred and Pt 3A (which applies only in England and Wales) with those which stir up religious hatred. Broadcasters and journalists also have to follow the codes of practice set out by Ofcom and the NUJ in relation to both racial and religious hatred.

RACIAL HATRED

"Racial hatred" is defined in s 17 of the Public Order Act 1986 as "hatred against a group of persons in Great Britain defined by reference to colour, race, nationality (including citizenship) or ethnic or national origins". Various offences can be committed under Pt 3 of the Act, but there is no requirement in any of them to show intention to stir up racial hatred, or that racial hatred actually took place. It only has to be shown that the accused was aware that this was likely to happen.

Under s 18 an offence is committed by the use of threatening, abusive or insulting words, or the displaying of them in written form, which are intended or likely to result in racial hatred. There are similar offences under ss 20 and 21. Section 21 relates to the distribution, showing or playing a recording of a visual image or sounds and s 20 to the public performances of plays.

Sections 19 and 22 are of more importance to the media. Section 19 makes it an offence either to publish or to distribute material that is threatening, abusive or insulting, and there has to be intention to stir up racial hatred or this has to be likely to occur, having regard to all the circumstances.

There is a defence under s 19(5) for an accused, who is not shown to have intended to stir up racial hatred, to prove that he was not aware of the content of the material and did not suspect, and had no reason to suspect, that it was threatening, abusive or insulting.

Sections 18 and 21 have similar defences to that provided for under s 19.

Section 22 of the Act covers the broadcasting of racially inflammatory material. It is an offence to use threatening, abusive or insulting images or sounds in a television programme or radio broadcast, including a cable service, intended or likely to stir up racial hatred. The offence can be committed by the producer of the programme, the director, the television company and any person "by whom the offending words or behaviour are used". It is not necessary to prove intention it can be shown that the programme content was in the circumstances likely to stir up racial hatred.

It is a defence under s 22(3), where the broadcaster, producer or director is not shown to have intended to stir up racial hatred, to show:

(1) that he did not know and had no reason to believe that the programme would involve the offending material; and

(2) that, having regard to the circumstances in which the programme was included in a programme service, it was not reasonable or practical for him to secure the removal of the material.

There is also a defence for producers and directors, where it is not proved that there was intention to cause racial hatred, if it can be shown that they had no reason to suspect:

(1) that the programme would be included in a programme service; or

(2) that the circumstances in which the programme would be so included would be such that racial hatred would be likely to be stirred up.

Under s 23 it is an offence to possess for publication or distribution certain material intended or likely to stir up racial hatred. There is a similar defence to that under s 19(5). Warrants can be granted for entry to and search of premises involved.

The 1986 Act does not affect fair and accurate reports of the proceedings of courts held in public and published contemporaneously, or reports of parliamentary proceedings.

RELIGIOUS HATRED

The Racial and Religious Hatred Act 2006 amended the Public Order Act 1986. Under Pt 3A of the 1986 Act (inserted by the 2006 Act), it is an offence under ss 29B, C, D, E and F intentionally to stir up hatred against persons on the ground of religion. The 2006 Act sets out the ways in which religious hatred may be incited. They are:

(1) the use of threatening words or behaviour or the display of threatening written material;

(2) publishing or distributing threatening written material;

(3) public performance of a play involving the use of threatening words;

(4) distributing, showing or playing a recording which includes threatening visual images or sounds; and

(5) broadcasting threatening visual or sound images.

These offences differ from racial ones in that, first, they can be committed only if there was intention to stir up religious hatred and, second, they do not include the words "insulting" and "abusive" but only have to be "threatening".

Section 29A defines "religious hatred" as "hatred against a group of persons defined by reference to religious belief or lack of religious belief".

Broadcasts

Under s 29F an offence is committed if a programme, involving threatening visual images or sounds, is included in a programme service and it is intended to stir up religious hatred. The persons liable under the section are;

(1) the person providing the programme service;

(2) any person by whom the programme is produced or directed; and

(3) any person by whom offending words or behaviour are used.

Where a corporation (s 29M), including a television or radio company, is guilty of an offence, a director, manager, secretary or other officer of the corporation will also be guilty if he consented to or connived in the commission of the offence.

Freedom of expression

To protect freedom of expression, s 29J provides that nothing in Pt 3A of the Act

"shall be read or given effect in a way which prohibits or restricts discussion, criticism or expressions of antipathy, dislike, ridicule, insult or abuse of particular religions or the beliefs or practices of their adherents, or of any other belief system or the beliefs or practices of its adherents, or proselytising or urging adherents of a different religion or belief system to cease practising their religion or belief system".

Possession and police powers

It is an offence to possess threatening material (s 29G), and the police have powers under the Act (s 29H) of entry and search where there are reasonable grounds for suspecting that a person is in possession of threatening inflammatory written material or threatening visual or sound recordings.

Reports

Section 29K gives protection to fair and accurate reports of court proceedings and reports of the UK and Scottish Parliaments.

Terrorism

The Terrorism Act 2006 criminalises the publication and dissemination of statements that glorify and encourage terrorism. A statement will be liable if it is likely "to be understood by some or all of the members of the public to whom it is published as a direct or indirect encouragement or other inducement to them to the commission, preparation or instigation of acts of terrorism or Convention offences".

Under s 1(2) a person will commit an offence if he publishes a statement or causes another to publish such a statement which, at the time of publication, was intended to encourage or otherwise induce members of the public, directly or indirectly, to commit, prepare or instigate acts of terrorism or Convention offences. Alternatively, the person will commit an offence if he was reckless as to the consequences of the publication.

It will depend on the content of the statement and the circumstances and manner of its publication whether or not it is likely to be understood as encouraging terrorism.

Statements that are likely to encourage terrorist acts are those which glorify the commission or preparation of terrorist acts or offences, or infer that what is being glorified should be emulated.

It is not relevant to the commission of the offence whether the publication relates to the commission of terrorist offences or actually encouraged any person to carry out an act of terrorism.

Section 2 of the 2006 Act deals with the dissemination of terrorist publications and is in similar terms to that of an offence under s 1 in the encouraging or inducing of terrorist acts. The dissemination of a terrorist publication includes the distributing, circulating, giving, selling or lending of a publication or transmitting the contents of it electronically.

There are defences under ss 1(9) and 2(9), where no intention can be shown, if the accused can prove:

(a) that the statement did not express his views or had his endorsement; and

(b) that it was clear from the circumstances that it did not express his views or have his endorsement.

Newspapers and broadcasters are therefore permitted to report this type of statement as long as it is quite clear that the views contained in the statement are not being endorsed or agreed with.

However, these defences are subject to s 3 of the Act which applies to statements published electronically. Failure to comply with a notice issued by a constable requiring a person to remove or modify threatening material from a website means that the person will have been deemed to have endorsed the statement. He must have been warned of the consequences and given an explanation that failure to do so will result in the commission of an offence. There is a defence to non-compliance with the notice if the person has taken every reasonable step to prevent a repeat statement from becoming available to the public.

The police can obtain a warrant to search for and remove any offending publications or other articles connected with the publication.

OBSCENE MATERIAL

The Civic Government (Scotland) Act 1982, s 51(1) makes it an offence to display any obscene material in any public place or in any place where it can be seen by the public. This includes any book, magazine, bill, paper, print, film, tape, disc or other kind of recording (whether of sound or visual images or both), photograph, drawing, painting, representation, model or figure. Under s 51(2), any person who publishes, sells or distributes obscene material, or keeps it, intending to do so, will be guilty of an offence. Persons responsible for the inclusion of obscene material in a programme included in a programme service, or who make, print or keep obscene material with a view to so including it, are also guilty of an offence under s 2A. There is a defence under s 56(4) if the person proves that he had used all due diligence to avoid committing the offence.

There is also a common law offence of shameless indecency which may be used to prosecute the publication or distribution of such material.

Under the Indecent Displays (Control) Act 1981 the display of indecent matter publicly (and this can include places to which the public have access, such as shops) is an offence. The 1981 Act does not apply to matter included by any person in a programme service.

7 PRIVACY

DEFINING PRIVACY

The right to privacy is a fundamental human right internationally recognised, most prominently in the Universal Declaration of Human Rights, the International Covenant on Civil and Political Rights and the European Convention on Human Rights. Although the UK is a founding signatory to the ECHR, the right to privacy was only incorporated into UK law in 1998 when the Human Rights Act was passed by Parliament.

However, the privacy right is often found in conflict with other interests and intrusion into one's privacy is allowed under the ECHR where it is necessary for the detection of crime or corruption or when national security is at stake, and, most contestedly, freedom of the media. Even in such instances, though, it is crucial that any invasion of a person's privacy is in direct proportion to any potential harm that would occur should the information be kept private. In other words, it should relate only to the private material necessary for the public interest. In cases where there is no public interest in disclosure, it is clear that the right to privacy is a vitally important, if not necessary, condition for human dignity and fulfilment and that it should be strictly upheld.

There is little argument that everyone should be entitled to keep their private life private as far as necessary to enable them to cultivate relationships with others, particularly intimate ones, and to maintain their physical and psychological well-being. However, it is extremely difficult to come to a clear conclusion on what the term means in a practical sense. Therefore privacy can reasonably be said to be difficult to define satisfactorily.

In fact, the problems associated with constructing a straightforward and understandable definition of "privacy" have been present since the notion of a right to privacy itself. By far the most prominent reason for this is the vast difference in human perceptions of their private life and affairs. A gross invasion for one individual can be normal, or even welcomed, by another. Each case will inevitably involve subtleties and a variety of circumstances that would be extremely difficult to anticipate in a legal sense. Quite simply, every case is different, and each individual involved is likely to have a different stance on how much, or how little, personal information they feel comfortable disclosing to others. Therefore a definition created from an objective viewpoint, without regard to context, environment or individual personality, is almost impossible.

This was highlighted in the case of *R v BSC, ex parte BBC* (2000), when Hale LJ stated: "Notions of what an individual might or might not want to be kept 'private', 'secret' or 'secluded' are subjective to that individual." Therefore, it can be suggested that an invasion of privacy arises only when an individual loses control over how much personal information they wish to disclose, ie when information is disclosed against their will as opposed to them volunteering the information themselves.

The invasion will inevitably occur when one is deprived of this choice. Despite the complexities surrounding the definition of the term, invasion of privacy is more prevalent in today's society than ever before. The modern day's increasing fascination with "celebrity" has bred a desire to know the most personal and intimate details about famous figures that would not have been acceptable in previous decades. Multiple new television programmes, newspapers and magazines have surfaced, increasing the competition for readers and audiences to the extent that only "newsworthy" articles are considered; typically, the most shocking or sensational stories prove most popular. This, alongside advances in technology, has propelled privacy to the forefront of any competent legal analysis of human rights.

PROTECTION OF PRIVACY IN THE UK

In the UK there had been no explicit recognition of a right to privacy until the Human Rights Act (hereafter "HRA") was enacted by Parliament in 1998. Traditionally, protection of privacy was afforded on the grounds of defamation, nuisance or trespass which involved privacy interest. Apparently, these actions were not *prima facie* concerned with privacy and therefore were not sufficient for the protection of privacy. The HRA incorporated the right of privacy, among others, as recognised under the European Convention on Human Rights, into the UK law. However, the enactment of the HRA does not enable individuals to sue the private media directly for an invasion of their privacy, as the HRA rights apply only to "public authorities" rather than "private individuals". It requires public authorities, including Parliament and the courts, to provide adequate protection of privacy in a way that is compatible with the Convention.

This also gives further effect to the right to freedom of expression, which brings the need for judges to "delicately balance" this with the right to privacy under Art 8 ECHR into domestic law. This can be seen in *Hellewell* v *Chief Constable of Derbyshire* (1995) in which photographs of a convicted shoplifter taken while he was in police custody were distributed to an organisation of shopkeepers who were concerned about the level of shoplifting in the area. The case was ultimately struck out when it was held that the actions of the police were "obviously and unarguably in the public interest" as they were reasonably directed to the prevention of crime; as such, distributing the photograph was held to be lawful, highlighting the frequently used "public interest" argument and so the need to weigh up the autonomy and privacy of an individual against any public interest that may lie in disclosing certain pieces of information and the freedom of expression on behalf of the defendant to disclose such information.

UK PARLIAMENT'S ATTEMPTS TO LEGISLATE

The UK legislature has, on several occasions, attempted to recognise the right to privacy in statute. However, this has consistently been without success and there is still no statutory protection in this field, other than the Human Rights Act which is interpreted solely by the courts and other piecemeal legislation, such as the Data Protection Act 1998.

The first legislative attempt was the "Right of Privacy" Bill which was introduced in the House of Lords in 1961. This Bill focused only on the "public disclosure" aspect of privacy and gained the support of Lord Denning. However, after the Second Reading, it was withdrawn due to lack of Government support. Following this, a second attempt was made to introduce a privacy law in 1967. Although this second Bill covered a wider range of privacy intrusion than the first, it failed at its First Reading. An investigation by a committee of JUSTICE into the failure of the common law to introduce such a right to privacy prompted another Bill to be introduced, this time in 1969. This Bill responded to the recommendation of the committee that there ought to be a "general right to privacy, applicable in all situations". However, it was argued at the Second Reading that this idea needed much clearer definition to ensure that people were aware of what types of activity were encompassed in the law as being "private". The recommendations made by the JUSTICE report were also met with a considerable degree of hostility, particularly from the media industry and the Press Council, who felt that, if incorporated into law, they would be extremely detrimental to freedom of speech and the all-important "free press". Other attempts to legislate have followed, including the privacy Bills in 1987 and 1989 – all of them unsuccessful.

Furthermore, several committees have, over the years, been given the task of considering the issue of whether a privacy law is required in the UK. The Younger Committee, formed in 1970, concluded that breach of confidence offered "the most effective protection of privacy in the whole of our existing law, civil and criminal". Sir David Calcutt, the chair of the Calcutt Committee which was formed in 1990 to consider the conduct of the Press in relation to privacy, warned that the Government "should now give further consideration to the introduction of a new tort of infringement of privacy". A statutory tribunal to consider privacy matters that had powers to penalise and award damages was also suggested, however, this suggestion was rejected by the National Heritage Select Committee, formed in 1992, which proposed another self-regulatory measure (the Press Commission) to enforce a new Press code.

NO PRIVACY DELICT/TORT IN COMMON LAW

It is long been recognised that there is no tort of privacy in the UK. Instead, the courts have been forced to act more imaginatively to provide a remedy using other existing common law torts. In *Kaye* v *Robertson* (1991) two journalists from the *Sunday Sport* entered television actor Gorden Kaye's hospital room and took photographs of him as he lay in bed injured, attached to a life-support machine after suffering a severe brain injury. They also made an attempt to interview him which proved unsuccessful because of his extremely confused state. Despite the court being sympathetic to Kaye's situation, it was unable to rule on an invasion of privacy since there was no tort of privacy in existence to protect a person's privacy. All other avenues, eg breach of confidence or trespass, were simply insufficient given the circumstances and so the only action available was malicious falsehood on the ground that the newspaper had given its readers the impression that Kaye had consented to the photographs being taken. The newspaper was ordered to publish an apology; however, this case highlighted the severe need for a privacy law applicable in situations where such an action would not be available:

> "It is well known that in English law there is no right to privacy, and accordingly there is no right of action for breach of a person's privacy. The facts of the present case are a graphic illustration of the desirability of Parliament considering whether and in what circumstances statutory provision can be made to protect the privacy of individuals."

PROTECTION OF PRIVACY UNDER OFCOM'S BROADCASTING CODE

Established in 2003, Ofcom oversees the practice of broadcasters and deals with the complaints of viewers and listeners in relation to, among other things, privacy. The legislation requires Ofcom to consider complaints about unwarranted infringement of privacy in a programme or in connection with the obtaining of material included in a programme. Accordingly, the Broadcasting Code provides detailed guidance on the rules instructing broadcasters to avoid infringement of privacy in various occasions. However, Ofcom recognises that broadcasters may have difficulties in making on-the-spot judgements about whether privacy is unwarrantably infringed by filming or recording, especially when reporting on emergency situations, and takes this into account when adjudicating on complaints. The basic principle of Ofcom is to ensure that broadcasters avoid any unwarranted infringement of privacy in programmes and avoid using those means of obtaining material that would intrude privacy. On the other hand, it allows broadcasters a public interest defence to an infringement of privacy as warranted where circumstances of the case justify the infringement. The Broadcasting Code provides examples of public interest, such as revealing or detecting crime, protecting public health or safety, exposing misleading claims made by individuals or organisations or disclosing incompetence that affects the public.

"* Broadcasting Code Section 8 (Excerpt)

PRIVATE LIVES, PUBLIC PLACES AND LEGITIMATE EXPECTATION OF PRIVACY

Meaning of 'legitimate expectation of privacy'

Legitimate expectations of privacy will vary according to the place and nature of the information, activity or condition in question, the extent to which it is in the public domain (if at all) and whether the individual concerned is already in the public eye. There may be circumstances where people can reasonably expect privacy even in a public place. Some activities and conditions may be of such a private nature that filming or recording, even in a public place, could involve an infringement of privacy. People under investigation or in the public eye, and their immediate family and friends, retain the right to a private life, although private behaviour can raise issues of legitimate public interest.

8.2 Information which discloses the location of a person's home or family should not be revealed without permission, unless it is warranted.

8.3 When people are caught up in events which are covered by the news they still have a right to privacy in both the making and the broadcast of a programme, unless it is warranted to infringe it. This applies both to the time when these events are taking place and to any later programmes that revisit those events.

8.4 Broadcasters should ensure that words, images or actions filmed or recorded in, or broadcast from, a public place, are not so private that prior consent is required before broadcast from the individual or organisation concerned, unless broadcasting without their consent is warranted.

Consent

8.5 Any infringement of privacy in the making of a programme should be with the person's and/or organisation's consent or be otherwise warranted.

8.6 If the broadcast of a programme would infringe the privacy of a person or organisation, consent should be obtained before the relevant material is broadcast, unless the infringement of privacy is warranted. (Callers to phone-in shows are deemed to have given consent to the broadcast of their contribution.)

8.7 If an individual or organisation's privacy is being infringed, and they ask that the filming, recording or live broadcast be stopped, the broadcaster should do so, unless it is warranted to continue.

8.8 When filming or recording in institutions, organisations or other agencies, permission should be obtained from the relevant authority or management, unless it is warranted to film or record without permission. Individual consent of employees or others whose appearance is incidental or where they are essentially anonymous members of the general public will not normally be required.

- However, in potentially sensitive places such as ambulances, hospitals, schools, prisons or police stations, separate consent should normally be obtained before filming or recording and for broadcast from those in sensitive situations (unless not obtaining consent is warranted). If the individual will not be identifiable in the programme then separate consent for broadcast will not be required.

Gathering information, sound or images and the re-use of material

8.9 The means of obtaining material must be proportionate in all the circumstances and in particular to the subject matter of the programme.

8.10 Broadcasters should ensure that the re-use of material, ie use of material originally filmed or recorded for one purpose and then used in a programme for another purpose or used in a later or different programme, does not create an unwarranted infringement of privacy. This applies both to material obtained from others and the broadcaster's own material.

8.11 Doorstepping for factual programmes should not take place unless a request for an interview has been refused or it has not been possible to request an interview, or there is good reason to believe that an investigation will be frustrated if the subject is approached openly, and it is warranted to doorstep. However, normally broadcasters may, without prior warning interview, film or record people in the news when in public places. (See 'practice to be followed' 8.15.)

Meaning of 'doorstepping'

Doorstepping is the filming or recording of an interview or attempted interview with someone, or announcing that a call is being filmed or recorded for broadcast purposes, without any prior warning. It does not, however, include vox-pops (sampling the views of random members of the public).

8.12 Broadcasters can record telephone calls between the broadcaster and the other party if they have, from the outset of the call, identified themselves, explained the purpose of the call and that the call is being recorded for possible broadcast (if that is the case) unless it is warranted not to do one or more of these practices. If at a later stage it becomes clear that a call that has been recorded will be broadcast (but this was not explained to the other party at the time of the call) then the broadcaster must obtain consent before broadcast from the other party, unless it is warranted not to do so. (See 'practices to be followed' 7.14 and 8.13 to 8.15.)

8.13 Surreptitious filming or recording should only be used where it is warranted. Normally, it will only be warranted if:

- there is prima facie evidence of a story in the public interest; and
- there are reasonable grounds to suspect that further material evidence could be obtained; and
- it is necessary to the credibility and authenticity of the programme.

(See 'practices to be followed' 7.14, 8.12, 8.14 and 8.15.)

Meaning of 'surreptitious filming or recording'

Surreptitious filming or recording includes the use of long lenses or recording devices, as well as leaving an unattended camera or recording device on private property without the full and informed consent of the occupiers or their agent. It may also include recording telephone conversations without the knowledge of the other party, or deliberately continuing a recording when the other party thinks that it has come to an end.

8.14 Material gained by surreptitious filming and recording should only be broadcast when it is warranted. (See also 'practices to be followed' 7.14 and 8.12 to 8.13 and 8.15.)

8.15 Surreptitious filming or recording, doorstepping or recorded 'wind-up' calls to obtain material for entertainment purposes may be warranted if it is intrinsic to the entertainment and does not amount to a significant infringement of privacy such as to cause significant annoyance, distress or embarrassment. The resulting material should not be broadcast without the consent of those involved. However if the individual and/or organisation is not identifiable in the programme then consent for broadcast will not be required. (See 'practices to be followed' 7.14 and 8.11 to 8.14.)

Suffering and distress

8.16 Broadcasters should not take or broadcast footage or audio of people caught up in emergencies, victims of accidents or those suffering a personal tragedy, even in a public place, where that results in an infringement of privacy, unless it is warranted or the people concerned have given consent.

8.17 People in a state of distress should not be put under pressure to take part in a programme or provide interviews, unless it is warranted.

8.18 Broadcasters should take care not to reveal the identity of a person who has died or of victims of accidents or violent crimes, unless and until it is clear that the next of kin have been informed of the event or unless it is warranted.

8.19 Broadcasters should try to reduce the potential distress to victims and/or relatives when making or broadcasting programmes intended to examine past events that involve trauma to individuals (including crime) unless it is warranted to do otherwise. This applies to dramatic reconstructions and factual dramas, as well as factual programmes.

- In particular, so far as is reasonably practicable, surviving victims and/ or the immediate families of those whose experience is to feature in a programme, should be informed of the plans for the programme and its intended broadcast, even if the events or material to be broadcast have been in the public domain in the past.

People under sixteen and vulnerable people

8.20 Broadcasters should pay particular attention to the privacy of people under sixteen. They do not lose their rights to privacy because, for example, of the fame or notoriety of their parents or because of events in their schools.

8.21 Where a programme features an individual under sixteen or a vulnerable person in a way that infringes privacy, consent must be obtained from:

- a parent, guardian or other person of eighteen or over in loco parentis; and
- wherever possible, the individual concerned;
- unless the subject matter is trivial or uncontroversial and the participation minor, or it is warranted to proceed without consent.

8.22 Persons under sixteen and vulnerable people should not be questioned about private matters without the consent of a parent, guardian or other person of eighteen or over in loco parentis (in the case of persons under sixteen), or a person with primary responsibility for their care (in the case of a vulnerable person), unless it is warranted to proceed without consent.

Meaning of 'vulnerable people'

This varies, but may include those with learning difficulties, those with mental health problems, the bereaved, people with brain damage or forms of dementia, people who have been traumatised or who are sick or terminally ill."

PRIVACY UNDER THE PRESS COMPLAINTS COMMISSION (PCC)

The PCC is a self-regulatory body funded by newspapers and magazines to regulate the industry by adjudicating complaints by members of the public against newspapers and magazines. It aims to deal with complaints but has no legal powers to enforce its decisions. It was established in the recognition that, whereas certain media practices towards individuals have led to demand for more statutory controls, the newspaper industry has sought to promote the virtues of self-regulation and stressed that its commitment to self-reglation makes it work effectively. Thus the PCC enacted the Code of Practice instructing newspaper journalists with regard to various aspects of journalistic activities. Among them, the provision on privacy is one of the most commonly invoked.

The main privacy rules are set out in cl 3 of the PCC Code of Practice, which states that "everyone is entitled to respect for his or her private and family life, home, health and correspondence, including digital communications", and "it is unacceptable to photograph individuals in a private place without their consent". It provides more specific rules, including requirements for the protection of children, grieving relatives, victims of sexual assault and patients in hospitals, as the following:

"5 **Intrusion into grief or shock**

    i) In cases involving personal grief or shock, enquiries and approaches must be made with sympathy and discretion and publication handled sensitively. This should not restrict the right to report legal proceedings, such as inquests.

    *ii) When reporting suicide, care should be taken to avoid excessive detail about the method used.

6 *Children

    i) Young people should be free to complete their time at school without unnecessary intrusion.

    ii) A child under 16 must not be interviewed or photographed on issues involving their own or another child's welfare unless a custodial parent or similarly responsible adult consents.

    iii) Pupils must not be approached or photographed at school without the permission of the school authorities.

    iv) Minors must not be paid for material involving children's welfare, nor parents or guardians for material about their children or wards, unless it is clearly in the child's interest.

    v) Editors must not use the fame, notoriety or position of a parent or guardian as sole justification for publishing details of a child's private life.

7 *Children in sex cases

    1. The press must not, even if legally free to do so, identify children under 16 who are victims or witnesses in cases involving sex offences.

    2. In any press report of a case involving a sexual offence against a child –

    i) The child must not be identified.

    ii) The adult may be identified.

    iii) The word 'incest' must not be used where a child victim might be identified.

    iv) Care must be taken that nothing in the report implies the relationship between the accused and the child.

8 *Hospitals

    i) Journalists must identify themselves and obtain permission from a responsible executive before entering non-public areas of hospitals or similar institutions to pursue enquiries.

    ii) The restrictions on intruding into privacy are particularly relevant to enquiries about individuals in hospitals or similar institutions.

9 *Reporting of crime

    i) Relatives or friends of persons convicted or accused of crime should not generally be identified without their consent, unless they are genuinely relevant to the story.

    ii) Particular regard should be paid to the potentially vulnerable position of children who witness, or are victims of, crime. This should not restrict the right to report legal proceedings.

10   ***Clandestine devices and subterfuge**

    i) The press must not seek to obtain or publish material acquired by using hidden cameras or clandestine listening devices; or by intercepting private or mobile telephone calls, messages or emails; or by the unauthorised removal of documents or photographs; or by accessing digitally-held private information without consent.

    ii) Engaging in misrepresentation or subterfuge, including by agents or intermediaries, can generally be justified only in the public interest and then only when the material cannot be obtained by other means.

11   **Victims of sexual assault**

The press must not identify victims of sexual assault or publish material likely to contribute to such identification unless there is adequate justification and they are legally free to do so."

With regard to defence to the intrusion of privacy, while Art 8 of the ECHR requires that the intrusion into private life must be justified in pursuant to legitimate aim and necessary and proportionate to the interests of public safety, health and morality, the prevention of crime or the rights of others in a democratic society, the PCC provides a broad scope for the intrusion into privacy as long as it is in line with the public interest. Under the Code, the intrusion into privacy is justified if:

- detecting or exposing crime or a serious misdemeanour;
- protecting public health and safety;
- preventing the public from being misled by some statement of action of an individual or organisation.

It also cites that where the public interest is invoked, the PCC will require editors to demonstrate fully how the public interest is served. The difficulty for the PCC is once again to strike a balance between privacy and the freedom of speech of the media. In practice, it appears that privacy complaints provoke more dispute and emotion than others arising from the Code.

In *A Woman* v *The News* (2004), a woman complained to the PCC that an article, headlined "Parents want to know how teacher got tuberculosis", published in *The News* on 13 February 2004, had identified her as a tuberculosis sufferer and thus intruded into her privacy in breach of cl 3 of the Code of Practice. The complaint was rejected. The newspaper ran a series of articles on the subject of the outbreak of tuberculosis at a local school, after the disease had been contracted by a teacher. The teacher contended that the newspaper should not have identified her without her consent. The PCC identified that the newspaper had made clear that the outbreak was extremely worrying for the local community. It was also noted that the newspaper had been told, in public announcements by relevant authorities, that the source of the outbreak was a Year 6 teacher, of which there were two in the school. As the complainant was the only Year 6 teacher on sick leave, hundreds of parents with children in the school were aware of her identity.

In *Riding* v *The Independent* (2006), Ms Joanna Riding complained to the PCC that an article published in *The Independent* on 8 March 2006 intruded into her privacy, in breach of cl 3. The article reported that the complainant had withdrawn from a theatre role because she had become pregnant. It said she had also pulled out from a previous role at the last minute because of a pregnancy. The complainant said the article intruded into her privacy by announcing her pregnancy before she had told even her family. The only people she had informed were her agent and the producer of the show. A Press release explaining her withdrawal referred only to unforeseen personal circumstances. The complainant subsequently suffered a miscarriage. The PCC considered that by revealing the complainant's pregnancy at such a stage, before she had told her family and when it was not obvious, was therefore a serious intrusion into her private life. The action taken and offered by the newspaper in response to the complaint was welcome but was not sufficient as a remedy to what was a significant breach of cl 3 of the Code. The Commission thus upheld the complaint.

The difficulties in keeping a balance between privacy and freedom of speech can, however, be shown more vividly in the inconsistency of the PCC's interpretations of the Code, in particular with regard to the "reasonable expectation of privacy" under cl 3. In *HRH Prince William* v *OK! Magazine* (2001), the Prince was photographed hiking on a public trial and fording a river at a public crossing during his gap year in Chile. The pictures were published in *OK!* magazine and the Palace made a complaint. The PCC decided that the Code was breached because he was on a trip "where he had a reasonable expectation of privacy". It additionally condemned the magazine for harassment, although there was not sufficient evidence that the photographer had come near the Prince. However, in *Stewart-Brady* v *Liverpool Echo and the Mirror* (2000), the "Moors Murderer" Ian Brady was photographed in the grounds of a hospital within a police van the curtains of which were open. The PCC dismissed the complaint on the basis that the picture was taken in an area of the hospital grounds which was open to the public.

That said, the PCC can operate, in terms of cost, as an efficient mechanism in affording protection of privacy, as no legal fees are to be paid for making a complaint and given the simple procedure the complaint can be swiftly responded to. The PCC also endeavours to improve the regime, making it more responsible to current concerns. Recently the PCC published guidelines on the Report on Subterfuge and Newsgathering (18 May 2007) as follows:

"• Contracts with external contributors should contain an explicit requirement to abide by the Code of Practice;

• A similar reference to the Data Protection Act should be included in contracts of employment;

• Publications should review internal practice to ensure that they have an effective and fully understood 'subterfuge protocol' for staff journalists, which includes who should be consulted for advice about whether the public interest is sufficient to justify subterfuge;

• Although contractual compliance with the Code for staff journalists is widespread, it should without delay become universal across the industry (the PCC will be pursuing this further);

• There should be regular internal training and briefing on developments on privacy cases and compliance with the law;

• There should be rigorous audit controls for cash payments, where these are unavoidable."

Essential Facts

• There is no common law delict/tort of privacy, therefore a claim for privacy is not actionable.

• Art 8 ECHR provides a right to respect for private and family life which covers privacy. The Human Right Acts 1998 incorporated this right into UK law.

• Ofcom affords protection of privacy under the Broadcasting Code and may impose administrative penalties on a broadcaster that violates the Code.

• The PCC is a self-regulatory body of newspapers and magazines which adjudicates on individuals' complaints against newspapers' or magazines' intrusions of their privacy. The PCC's decision, however, is not legally binding.

Essential Case

Kaye v Robertson (1991): the court held that there was no common law tort of privacy. This case shows the inadequacy of UK law in protecting privacy before the HRA was enacted in 1998.

8 BREACH OF CONFIDENCE

In the absence of any general law to protect privacy in the UK, a common law delict/tort of breach of confidence has consistently been used to provide remedies in this area. Breach of confidence is a civil remedy which affords protection for individuals against disclosure of information that has been entrusted to another party in circumstances that create a relationship of confidence. In other words, if there exists an obligation not to disclose the information, subsequent disclosure would be a breach of confidence and subject to such an action in the courts.

The first ever breach of confidence is thought to date back to 1849, in *Prince Albert* v *Strange*. Since this case the doctrine of breach of confidence has grown rapidly, as have the arguments for and against a separate privacy tort. At the moment, any individual wishing to make a claim for intrusion of privacy must exercise such under the law of breach of confidence.

It should be noted that there is a significant difference between confidential information and information which is private. A good example of confidential information is the business secret of a company which employees are obliged not to release to other parties without the consent of the company. In this case the information is confidential but not private. Many relationships are subject to a duty of confidence. These relationships are usually domestic, contractual and legal; however, the relationships included in this principle have been expanded over the years and many more are now questioned through the courts than ever before. On the other hand, there are cases in which information is private but not confidential; for instance, a picture in which a person is seen in an unfavourable position in a far-off corner of a park. The photographer does not have an obligation of confidence to this person, so he may release the picture to the media. Nonetheless, in most cases there is an overlap between confidential information and privacy, such as details about private married life which a husband and wife are obliged not to disclose to others without the consent of the other party.

It should also be noted that the changing attitudes towards the obligation of confidence have shifted over the last few decades. The principle was once clearly defined up until now when the application of such principle is being overly used. In the well-known case *Coco* v *A N Clark (Engineers) Ltd* (1968), the Lords created and listed three key elements necessary within a case to satisfy a claim for breach of confidence. These are:

- the information must have the necessary quality of confidence about it;
- it must have been imparted in a situation within which there was an obligation of confidence; and
- the information imparted had to then be used to the detriment of the person who communicated it initially.

For the first condition, the necessary quality of confidence, the topic or subject-matter must be of the correct significance to be recognised as a confidence and not to be trivial. However, this necessity has been subject to great development since *Coco*. Initially it was accepted that the information, if known that it was confidential by the recipient, would be unconscionable to uncover.

The second key element of breach of confidence is that the relationship, or indeed situation, in which the confidential information was imparted must be necessary for the courts to protect it. The confidential relationship does not have to be marital or even heterosexual, although marriage is often used as an example. The only necessity is that the relationship carries a duty of confidence. If this is proven, the person to whom the confidential information is being imparted will be under a duty to keep it protected and not to make it publicly known in any way. The array of relationships which carry a duty of confidence has been expanded over the years, from a relationship of marriage to a homosexual relationship. In *Barrymore* v *News Group Newspapers Ltd* (1997), Michael Barrymore was able to obtain an injunction to stop the *Sun* newspaper from printing information obtained by interviewing his former lover. The recognition that homosexual relations are now confidential relations is enabling the law to keep up with society's ever-changing values. The conclusion that can be drawn from this principle is that the relationship can be of any form so long as the courts accept that there was, at some point in time, a confidence between both parties, whether this be of an intimate relationship or merely a strong friendship.

Away from the domestic setting, there are also other relationships that are subject to a confidence that may not involve only two parties. There can be a confidential relationship between government bodies and any civil servants working within a contract. The Official Secrets Acts place restrictions on any member of staff working for the Government from revealing its secrets. The most famous case regarding this principle is *Attorney-General* v *Guardian Newspapers Ltd* (1990). It was recognised here that, once published and internationally known, the newspapers cannot be prohibited from publishing confidential information which the public may easily access elsewhere.

The third and final principle set out in *Coco* was determined on the basis that the confidential information had been used in some way to the detriment of the affected party. If this principle was absolute then it would have to be proven that a negative effect impacted on the party's life in some way. However, for people using breach of confidence as a remedy, this principle is not absolute and it has even been shown in later cases that no detriment need exist in order successfully to sue for breach of confidence. It is thought that breach of confidence does still exist whether or not harm has come to the person seeking to protect their private affairs. Anonymity should be a privilege one is able to decide for oneself – not for others to determine whether it should be kept or not.

There are, of course, times when the principles mentioned in *Coco* will not stand. The defences in relation to this include when the information is already in the public domain; when the information is in the public interest and this interest overrules any obligation of confidence; and finally when the information is so trivial that, although imparted in confidential circumstances, it is of such unimportance that it would not be in the court's interest to bother with it.

The first defence mentioned is that the information is already in the public domain. This defence has been created over the years and has much case law surrounding it. A media organisation or publishing authority has the right to publish any information, including confidential information, if it is commonly known or has already been published elsewhere such that a percentage of the public is already aware of it. Some restrictions are placed on the "public domain defence". The previous publication or indeed the existence of a public record is a deciding factor in the public domain defence but not a conclusive one. The Law Commission has also been seen to suggest that information published locally some time ago should not preclude the protection against that same information being published widely at a later date. For the public domain defence to apply, information should be regarded as such only if it is generally available to the public. No great skill, labour or money need be expended to retrieve the information.

The defence of public interest was created to allow media organisations to publish information which ought to be drawn to the public's attention. Confidential information would be permitted to be disclosed if this would serve the public interest. This is when the public interest outweighs the need to preserve the information. It was once believed that the courts would protect only "iniquity", and that a confidence could be breached in order to expose some sort of wrongdoing. This general thought has, however, been extended over the years to protect the public from certain confidences and also by disclosing the information it believes is in its interest. This is done by balancing the two to provide an outcome of what is best for the public at large. There has been a change to what is accepted as a public interest defence. There have been many recent cases whereby no iniquity is involved but still the courts believe there to be a strong public interest defence. In *Lion Laboratories Ltd* v *Evans* (1984), it was highlighted by the court that one must be very careful not to confuse matters of public interest with matters that are interesting to the public. Of course, it is easy to note that in the culture in which we live, celebrity lifestyles and their private relations may be of interest to the public but it would not be in the public interest to disclose such information. It can also be noted that the extent of disclosure should be in the public's interest. If it is suitable enough to disclose only part of the private information then this is all that will be necessary; there would be no need to disclose confidential information any further than required.

The law of breach of confidence provides remedies for those wishing to, for example, prohibit publication of their private lives or any confidential information they shared with someone close to them. Breach of confidence, now used as a privacy remedy, has been changed and may even be considered to be distorted over time to suit invasion of privacy claims. Breach of confidence no longer has the same requirements as it traditionally did and does not require the same standard of interpretation. In *Douglas* v *Hello! Ltd* (2003), the judges favoured the option to extend confidentiality to situations where the intruder had no special relationship with the claimant. This expansion of breach of confidence can be most notably seen in the courts' decisions in the wake of the Human Rights Act 1998.

DEVELOPMENT OF BREACH OF CONFIDENCE IN THE POST-HRA ERA

Protection of privacy now seems to be a growing right which, to many, has been long awaited. One of the most cited and maybe most influential cases regarding protection of privacy is *Campbell* v *Mirror Group Newspapers* (2004). In this case it was relevant to note that the courts stepped away from the traditional method of dealing with a breach of confidence case and focused primarily on whether or not Naomi Campbell's privacy had been intruded. One of the most interesting facts of the case was the type of information that was considered to be confidential or not.

The publication included both photographs and a reporter's article regarding the plaintiff leaving a drug rehabilitation centre. The reporter believed this to be an important article to publish because of the right of the public to know that a public figure was lying to them. Ms Campbell had previously been denying that she had any drug problem or addiction. It was, in the eyes of the reporter, important to alert the public to the lies that they had been told. The House of Lords, on a 3–2 basis, eventually agreed that the test to be considered was whether the information would be substantially offensive to a "reasonable" person, assuming that person was placed in similar circumstances. It was agreed by the House that the public did have a right to know the truth, in respect that Ms Campbell did have a drug problem and had lied. It was, however, held that the unit where she was receiving her treatment was where the invasion into her privacy lay. The court seemed to recognise that public figures should indeed expect a lower degree of protection of their privacy than the average man; how far the Press is able to delve into a public figure's private life is still a matter of contention, mainly because of the interest that the public do have over figures in the public eye.

With *Campbell* it has been proven that the House of Lords is happy to approve the protection of privacy through breach of confidence by blurring the demarcation line between confidence and privacy. One issue to highlight from *Campbell* is the protection afforded to individuals when they are in a public place. The protection afforded to individuals in public places will be discussed in relation to *von Hannover* in the next section; however, it does seem that the courts are often likely to take different approaches when the published information is photographic. This may be seen by some as too intrusive and this is highlighted in cases whereby the judges have prohibited the publication of such photographs but have allowed the story, or in other words the detailed account of events, to be published freely. When it comes to photographs which portray a mood and a person's demeanour and give the complete description of that individual, it seems that the line into intrusion is crossed.

More recently, the UK courts have taken on board the high importance that should be attached to privacy. The very recent case of *Mosley* v *News Group* (2008) has led to great debate, as the outcome of the case saw Mosley awarded the highest sum of compensatory damages in a privacy case to date. Mosley was able to convince the judge, Eady J, that he had a reasonable expectation of privacy and that the group within which he was seen relied heavily upon confidentiality and that their expectations must be respected. The main problem with this case was determining whether or not the conduct highlighted in newspapers and magazines was of great public interest. Should this behaviour have been protected against invasion by the Press or was the Press entitled to freely express its opinions? The judge studied and made reference to the argument put forward by the newspapers. News Group stated that the public interest defence applied because of the allegations of criminality within the sado-masochist acts taking place. Within the judgment Eady J referred to the *Campbell* case and highlighted that the only reason disclosure had been allowed there was that Campbell had previously lied about her situation and misled the public, not because the conduct was illegal. It was held that the situation in which Mosley was caught was not illegal but, even if it had been, it is presumed that a similar outcome would have still been decided. Eady J stated that "indulging in illegal behaviour does not automatically undermine a person's right to privacy". Although used only in defamation cases, it was considered whether the reporter had used reasonable journalism within the context of the *Mosley* case. Eady J concluded that the journalist had made no attempt to verify the authenticity of the conduct nor had he tried to understand the information upon which he relied heavily in order to make accusations. It was stated that the journalist's work was "erratic and changeable" and did not meet the requirements for responsible journalism.

Mosley has not been the only case to draw great attention on the privacy front. Only months earlier than *Mosley*, the following case brought invasion of privacy back to the forefront of discussion: *Murray v Express Newspapers Plc and Big Pictures (UK) Ltd* (2008). The main difference in this case is that Mr and Mrs Murray (the author J K Rowling and her husband) were claiming for invasion of privacy because of family photographs being taken, without permission, which showed their 19-month-old son in great detail, highlighting his clothes, hair, profile and skin colour. In the initial case the judge dismissed the Murrays' action to stop publication of the photograph: Patten J believed that if a simple walk down the street could be held as private then there would be very little which would not be protected in future. The decision was subsequently appealed and the court stated something very different from the initial case. The Court of Appeal held that the Murrays had an arguable case that they had a reasonable expectation of privacy and an arguable case that the balance between Art 8 and Art 10 of the European Convention of Human Rights should be struck in their favour.

The expansion of the law of confidence suggests that it is necessary to move towards a full right to privacy, as most notably demonstrated in *Wainwright* v *UK* (2007), where Wainwright and her son were strip-searched when visiting her other son in a prison, which she claimed was a violation of her Art 8 right. After her claim for privacy was turned down by the UK courts, Ms Wainwright appealed to the European Court of Human Rights. That court held that the UK was not able to provide a sufficient remedy and was thus in violation of Art 8 ECHR.

EUROPEAN COURT OF HUMAN RIGHTS' APPROACH

The European Convention for the Protection of Human Rights and Fundamental Freedoms, drafted in the aftermath of the Second World War, sought to create an international standard of rights and freedoms that could not be ignored or denied by the state. It is clear that the intention of the Council of Europe, when drafting the Convention, was to prevent a repeat of the humanitarian abuses that occurred during the war, in particular the Holocaust. Among the rights it enshrines is the right to privacy. This is laid out in Art 8 which states that "everyone has the right to respect for his private and family life, his home and his correspondence" and that "there shall be no interference by a public authority with the exercise of this right except such as is in accordance with the law and is necessary in a democratic society".

This article protects an individual's rights in two separate ways. First, it entitles everyone, regardless of their gender, race, religion or political views, to respect for their private and family life, their home and correspondence. Second, it places an obligation on public authorities not to interfere with this right, subject to the exceptions given. However, at this juncture it is important to note the use of the term "respect for" rather than "privacy". This terminology indicates that, in the absence of a consistent understanding of the limits of privacy as a general right, the Convention is attempting to ensure that a person's right to autonomy and dignity are respected so far as a reasonable person would consider acceptable.

On the other hand, any interference with a person's privacy can be deemed acceptable if it falls under one of the exceptions given in the Convention, one of these being "for the protection of the rights and freedoms of others". This exception can clearly apply to the right to freedom of expression under Art 10 which includes the "freedom to hold opinions and to receive and impart information and ideas".

Free speech, particularly in the realm of Press freedom, is held in high regard at Strasbourg. It has been stated that freedom of expression constitutes one of the essential foundations of a democratic society and that it is applicable not only to "information" or "ideas" that are favourably received or regarded as inoffensive but also to those that offend, shock or disturb.

Despite the long-standing view that freedom of expression is a vitally important human need, particularly with regard to the discovery of truth, this right is often found in conflict with other rights, particularly with the right to privacy. Although Art 10 is subject to exceptions, including a need for the protection of the reputation or the rights of others which plainly observes the right to an individual's private life, it has consistently been argued that freedom of expression and privacy represent conflicting concepts that must be delicately balanced in order to avoid unfair preference for one or the other. In other words, the goal must be finding and maintaining that perfect, delicate balance between "freedom to" and "freedom from".

In response to the view that allowing the media freely to disclose information about public figures to their audience or readers is a breach of privacy, it can be argued that, as invasions of privacy concern truthful facts, it is the right of the public to know what public bodies are doing if it is in their interest. The so-called "public watchdog" that is the Press, acting in the interests of the public, is one of the most important aspects of any democracy. However, it has long been recognised that there is a wide difference between what is interesting to the public and what it is in the public interest to make known.

The concept of allowing a margin of appreciation when considering actions of Member States with regard to Convention rights has developed substantially over time, to become a fundamental doctrine in the jurisprudence in the European Court, and now plays a central role in the majority of cases the Court decides.

The doctrine affords a certain leeway to be to given to Member States when deciding on cases regarding an incompatibility with Convention rights. The ECtHR decides whether the exercise of the discretion is compatible with the ECHR. (For a comprehensive discussion on the margin of appreciation doctrine, see Fenwick and Phillipson, *Media Freedom under the Human Rights Act* (2006), Chapter 13.)

In essence, this doctrine operates to avoid any suggestion that the Court is "trespassing" on a state's sovereignty in any given decision. It is important to ensure that the obligation to uphold citizens' rights falls primarily on the state itself and, because of this, the task of the Court is simply to examine any action or decision made by the Member State and conclude whether or not this is compatible with the Convention. In doing so, as mentioned, a level of discretion will be afforded to the state involved. The amount of discretion, ie a wider or narrower margin of appreciation, will be applied depending on the individual circumstances in the case. A variety of criteria exists to determine the "width" of the margin. A wide margin will be afforded in situations where the complainant seeks to lay a positive obligation on the state in question, or where the harm is inflicted by a private party rather than the state itself, or when there is a potential conflict with another Convention right. However, a narrower margin can be applied in situations where there is a substantial agreement among Member States on a particular issue or, in general, where the nature of the Convention right in question is such that a narrower margin is deemed appropriate. Obviously, it is for the Court to interpret whether a wider or narrower margin ought to be afforded but the custom in affording a wide margin in cases involving privacy has led to some controversial judgments in this area. This statement is particularly true for invasion of privacy because, generally, most, or indeed all, of the above-mentioned criteria needed for a wide margin to be applied are present in privacy cases against the private media.

Despite the possibility for misleading and inconsistent rulings, a need for latitude in court rulings is necessary, if not vitally important. Because of the requirement on Member States to have regard to decisions of the Court, having jurisdiction in a large variety of cases from different countries, all with different cultures, societies and laws, is not something that can be done rigidly. Allowances must be made for the current standards and legal principles in each Member State. In other words, the Convention must be given an "evolutive interpretation" which takes into account the laws in each Member State and interprets their actions appropriately. An example of the vast discrepancy between states can be seen very clearly in the area of privacy. While France offers its citizens a high level of protection against unwanted intrusion by the Press, the UK offers a distinctly lower level of protection. In decisions made by the Court, these contrasting standards must be taken into account.

There is nothing in the Convention to suggest that an over-arching right to privacy in general is necessary for compatibility with the Convention. Furthermore, the second part of this right – that interference by a public body is, in most circumstances, forbidden – does not cover the application of the right from a private or social standpoint.

For this reason the European Court has been cautious in finding that there is a subsequent requirement on Member States to develop a remedy for invasion of privacy by a private individual or body, such as the largely privately owned media industry. In fact, it was only very recently, in the decision in *von Hannover* v *Germany* (2004), that the long-standing confusion over whether such a remedy ought to exist was answered.

Originally, such a requirement, albeit a loose one, did appear to be necessary in *X and Y* v *The Netherlands* (1985) in which the Court held that the obligations under Art 8 "may require the adoption of measures even in the sphere of relations between individuals"; however, in *Winer* v *UK* (1986), a different picture emerged. In this case it was claimed that an invasion of privacy had occurred in relation to the disclosure of truthful personal information in the book *Inside Boss*. The applicant had previously settled a case on defamation with regard to some of the statements made in the book and was attempting to claim breach of privacy for the other statements. This claim was held to be inadmissible because it was found that there was no positive obligation on the Member State to provide any further remedies than they already had done, as doing so would be detrimental to the conflicting right of freedom of expression. The remedies available for defamation were held to be adequate to compensate for the breach of privacy. Although this decision rejected the idea that the state was required to implement measures specifically for the protection of privacy beyond the remedies already available, as had been previously suggested in *X and Y*, and did not attempt satisfactorily to distinguish a person's right to privacy from their right to reputation, the perception of the Court's approach to privacy protection was believed to be that the issue of breach of privacy is inherently subject to a very wide margin of appreciation and, as such, Member States were not required to provide a specific privacy remedy for individuals whose privacy had been, within reason, breached by another private individual.

However, as it was held in *Winer* that sufficient alternative remedies were available, the decision presented the possibility of an obligation being imposed on the state to provide a remedy for a breach of privacy in cases where there is no other remedy available. This possibility was later supported in *N* v *Portugal* (1995), when the Commission rejected the application of a magazine publisher who complained that his right to freedom of expression had been violated after he had been held to breach a well-known businessman's privacy in publishing pictures of him engaged in sexual activities. It was held that the sentence imposed on the publisher was "proportionate and necessary" in order to protect the rights of others.

Furthermore, the case of *Earl Spencer* v *UK* (1998), which concerned the publication in tabloid newspapers of photographs and information regarding Countess Spencer's time in a clinic for treatment of her eating disorder and alcoholism, seemed to find that, not only could the privacy of individuals be breached by other private individuals, but that effective remedies need to be provided by Member States to prevent this. In this case the PCC had stated that there had been a breach of cl 3 of its Code of Practice, however upon application to the Commission it was held that because the Spencers had not "exhausted their domestic remedies" they could not bring the case in the European Court. This was because there were adequate remedies available to them under the law of confidence in the UK, which they had not used. In this case, it was held there was a breach of privacy, but a very wide margin of appreciation was applied and it seems to suggest that, far from not having adequate remedies in this area, the Court believes the UK already has sufficient protection for invasions of privacy in place.

In *Peck* v *UK* (1998) the situation slightly improved for privacy protection by private bodies. Mr Peck, who was suffering from depression at the time, attempted to commit suicide with a kitchen knife while walking alone down Brentwood High Street. A CCTV camera operator picked up on him walking along the street with the knife and, understandably, alerted the police to apprehend him. The police arrived, gave Mr Peck medical assistance and brought him to the police station where he was detained under the Mental Health Act. After examination by a doctor, he was released without charge and escorted home. In the following months several articles, newspapers and television programmes reported on the incident, some of which failed specifically to mask the applicant's face. Once Mr Peck had become aware that his image was being used in such a way, he complained to the Council who had originally disclosed the CCTV images. The Council assured him that his face would be masked in the main *Crime Beat* programme but it was left unmasked in the related adverts in the programme and so he was still recognised by friends and family. After several media appearances to speak out about the publication of the footage, he complained to the Broadcasting Standards Commission (BSC) who upheld his objections, as did the ITC (now Ofcom) and an apology was issued. However, after this his complaint to the Press Complaints Commission (PCC) and his application for judicial review of the Council's actions to the High Court were both rejected, he lodged his application with the European Commission of Human Rights on 22 April 1996. The European Court observed that particular scrutiny was needed because of the inherent "crime prevention objective" but held that the disclosure of the footage and images was a "disproportionate and unjustified interference with the applicant's private life and a violation of Article 8". It was also found that Mr Peck's media appearances afterwards did not diminish his claim as he was "the victim of a serious interference with his right to privacy" and it could not be held against him that he later attempted to expose the wrongdoings of the media and the Council. This decision makes it clear that the media can breach the privacy of others, and that remedies must be provided, however, in this case it was the disclosure of the footage by the Council that primarily breached Mr Peck's privacy and the broadcasting of such footage by the BBC, which logically comes under the definition of "public authority" in Art 8. No definite answer was given to whether such disclosure and broadcasting would engage Art 8 if carried out by a non-public authority. However, based on the decision in *Earl Spencer* v *UK*, it would appear that it would, but Peck would have only the action of breach of confidence available to him.

Importantly, this decision was made with reference to context. As Peck was involved in an incident that it can be assumed he would prefer to have been kept private (an attempted suicide) and, as stated in the ruling, that the material was broadcast to a "much wider audience than he could have possibly foreseen", it was a clear breach of privacy. The context and nature of the material are vitally important when considering whether images or footage breach privacy because of the potential conflicts with Art 10. However, it can be seen from the recent case law that Europe is becoming extremely liberal in its judicial approach to Art 8. This is particularly because of the ruling in *von Hannover* v *Germany* (2004). This case involved Princess Caroline von Hannover of Monaco, a well-known royal figure. As a consequence of her fame, photographs were regularly taken of her and her children when out in public, while she was not in the process of carrying out her public functions. She was followed and harassed by photographers on a regular basis. The importance of the underlying values of privacy, dignity, autonomy and liberty was discussed in depth in this case and it was held that the media attention had sufficiently invaded Princess Caroline's privacy in respect of Art 8. It was decided that, despite being in a public place, she was engaged in "activities of a purely private nature" and so she was entitled to a "legitimate expectation" that her private life would be protected.

This case made it unmistakably clear that Art 8 is engaged by the private media and also that remedies must be provided in respect of this. As a result, the scope of privacy appears to have been greatly extended, regardless of the confusion over this issue just a few years earlier. Despite the German courts providing a remedy for the more intrusive pictures taken of the Princess, they were still held to have breached Art 8 by not providing a remedy for *all* of the pictures, even though the remaining pictures were simply of her partaking in normal, everyday activities. Interestingly, the nature of the material, something that was highly regarded in *Peck*, appears not to have been used in this decision and there has subsequently been no explanation of why the Court has chosen to extend the scope of Art 8 so dramatically and substantially reduce any margin of appreciation used. However, it can also be inferred that the particular circumstances in the case, ie the constant harassment of photographers and the unrelenting way in which the photos were taken, creating a "climate of continual harassment", had an important bearing on the judgment. If this is the case, then it is not necessarily the activities that the photographs portray that intrudes upon the Princess's private life, but rather the environment in which they were taken. Unfortunately, the Court does not express what the decisive factor in this case was and so, yet again, its ruling is open to interpretation.

Nevertheless, the approach of the Court towards privacy cases is now extremely wide. This can be seen in the recent case of *Reklos and Davourlis v Greece* (2009), in which it seems to have been extended even further. In this case professional photographs were taken of a new-born baby boy in an Athens hospital, as part of the hospital's photography service offered to clients. The parents of the child objected to these photographs being taken without their consent and requested that the negatives be handed over to them. When this was refused they brought an action for damages in the Athens Court of First Instance. Their action, at this stage, was dismissed. They attempted to appeal twice more, on the merits of the case as well as on points of law, however both attempts were unsuccessful. The Court observed in this case that the concept of "private life" was extremely broad and included within it the right to identity. It concluded that an image reveals the "unique characteristics" about a person – these characteristics being a main part of their individual personality. It was held that whether or not the pictures were ultimately published, consent should be sought before taking the photograph, as doing so without permission constituted an invasion of a person's identity and thus their privacy. As the child was a minor, the photographer ought to have asked for the parents' permission before taking the picture. This permission was not given, nor asked for, and the European Court ruled that the Greek courts in this instance had not taken sufficient steps to guarantee their citizens' right to privacy under Art 8 of the Convention.

Essential Facts

- The traditional doctrine of breach of confidence established that three conditions had to be met in order to bring an action of breach of confidence: the information must have the quality of confidence; there is an explicit or implied obligation of confidence; and the use of confidential information must not be authorised.

- The courts developed a new stance on breach of confidence in *Campbell* v *MGN* (so-called "*Campbell* confidence") which amends the traditional doctrine. "Campbell confidence" expands the scope of confidential information and disregards whether there is an existing obligation of confidence.
- European Court of Human Rights gives domestic courts of the Member States a margin of appreciation in implementing Art 8 ECHR.

Essential Cases

Coco v A N Clark (Engineers) Ltd (1968): established a traditional doctrine of breach of confidence by listing three key elements necessary within a case to satisfy a claim for breach of confidence: (1) the information must have the necessary quality of confidence about it; (2) the information must have been imparted in a situation within which there was an obligation of confidence; (3) the information imparted had to then be used to the detriment of the person who communicated it initially.

Campbell v Mirror Group Newspapers (2004): developed the traditional doctrine of breach of confidence by expanding the scope of confidential information and disregarding confidential relationship as essential. It applied a "reasonable expectation test" for privacy.

von Hannover v Germany (2004): the European Court of Human Rights took a broad view of privacy and held that activities of a purely private nature in public places which fall within reasonable expectation of privacy are entitled to the protection of Art 8 ECHR.

9 COPYRIGHT

DEFINITION AND SCOPE OF COPYRIGHT

"Copyright" is the term used to describe the rights granted by law to the author of a work to protect that work against unauthorised use such as publishing or reproducing it without the permission of the copyright owner. It is a legal framework for the protection of a series of intangible rights which do not have physical substance. Copyright protects not only the intellectual property in the work, ie the product of a person's imagination and creativity, but also the copyright owner's right to control how their work is used and to generate an income from it. By doing so, copyright law encourages individual effort by rewarding personal gain in order to stimulate artistic creativity for the general public good; it also makes reward to individuals for the labour and skills they executed in creating works.

However, it should be kept in mind that one of the fundamental properties of copyright law is that only expressions are protected, not ideas. For example, while the plot, dialogue, images etc of the film *The Day after Tomorrow* are protected by copyright because these are all expressions of an idea, the idea of the disastrous impacts of global warming on the environment is not protected. This property of copyright law, and the distinction between ideas and expressions, is often referred to as the "idea–expression dichotomy". In *Baigent and Leigh* v *Random House* (2006), Michael Baigent and Richard Leigh, who in 1982 wrote a book called *The Holy Blood and the Holy Grail*, claimed that *The Da Vinci Code*, written by Dan Brown and published by Random House, breached their copyright by copying the central theme of their book without permission. Both books explore the theory that Jesus and Mary Magdalene had a child and that the bloodline survives to this day. The court held that Dan Brown did use scenes in the previous book to write certain parts of his thriller but did not substantially copy Baigent and Leigh's work.

In the UK, copyright is granted automatically once the author completes the work, unless it is subject to other factors, for example contract law. Copyright exists only when the work is fixed in any material form. In the UK it does not have to be formally registered, as in other countries such as the US. However, an author can mark the work with the symbol "©", his name and the date of creation, though this is not legally necessary and is not a legal test of copyright ownership. The owner of a copyright has certain exclusive rights regarding copying, dissemination, communication to the public, public performance and adaptation of the original work, which last for the duration of the author's life plus an additional 70 years for literary, dramatic, musical and artistic works and films. In addition, the author has certain moral rights regarding the subject of copyright, which include the right to be recognised as the original author ("right of paternity") and the right for the work to be unaltered without permission and acknowledgment ("right of integrity"). Recognising the importance of access to copyrighted works in the interest of the public, copyright law provides two major defences to copyright infringement; first, "permitted acts", more commonly known as "fair dealing", which constitute copying works for the purposes of private study, research, criticism, review or newspaper summary. Fair dealing with a work does not require the permission of the copyright owner or the payment of royalties. The second defence to infringement is termed "public interest", where the work is deemed important for wider distribution.

A number of pieces of UK legislation deal with copyright, the most important being the Copyright, Designs and Patents Act (CDPA) 1988, and there are also international agreements that protect copyright of the authors of one country in other Member States, such as the Berne Convention, the World Intellectual Property Organization Copyright Treaty and the WTO Agreement on Trade-related Aspects of Intellectual Property. The EU also harmonises copyright and intellectual property legislation throughout the Member States, mainly via the Copyright Directive (2001/29/EC)

SUBJECT-MATTER OF COPYRIGHT

The CDPA provides a number of categories of subject-matters to be protected according to the nature of the works.

- *Literary works*: including books, journal articles, short stories, poems, manuals, lyrics to songs, a table or compilation expressed in words, figures, symbols, computer programs, newspaper articles, reports, sets of instructions, any practical or information lists.
- *Artistic works*: including paintings, sculptures, drawings (including diagrams, maps, charts and plans, dress patterns), cartoons, engravings (including etchings, lithographs, products of photogravure, woodcut prints or similar works), photographs, buildings or models of buildings, works of artistic craftsmanship (ceramics etc).

- *Dramatic works*: including plays, television, radio and film scripts, scenarios and other works intended to be performed such as choreographic notations, even where the work does not include spoken words, eg mime, dance.
- *Musical works*: including notated music such as musical scores for opera, operetta, orchestral, ensemble, band and other musical performances as well as music for songs.
- *Films*: including documentaries, feature and animated films, TV programmes, commercials, video tapes and cassettes and other fixed or recorded sequences of visual images. The visual images and film are protected separately to any copyright in works recorded on the film or video such as scripts and music.
- *Sound recordings*: including phonograms, compact discs, audio tapes, cassettes and other fixed or recorded sounds. Sound recordings include recorded music as well as recorded words and sounds.
- *Broadcasts of television and radio programmes*: ie broadcast signals, copyright in which is separate to the copyright in the films, music and other material which is transmitted.
- *Typographic arrangements of literary, dramatic or musical works*: where copyright of the works has expired and is in the public domain, eg a novel by Jane Austen, copyright applies to the published edition but protects only the typographical arrangement and layout.

EXCLUSIVE RIGHTS

The authors of works protected by copyright, heirs of their copyright, or anyone who acquired copyright from an author are granted certain exclusive rights that have economic significance. Copyright owners have the exclusive right to use or authorise others to use the work on agreed terms. They can prohibit or authorise its reproduction in various forms, such as printed publication or sound recording; its public performance, as in a play or musical work; recordings of it, for example in the form of compact discs, cassettes or video tapes; its broadcasting, by radio, cable or satellite; its translation into other languages; or its adaptation, such as from a novel into a screenplay. Under the CDPA there are five categories of exclusive rights:

- *Right of copying/reproduction* of works in various forms, such as printed publication or sound recording, to make any copies of the work in any form or method, for example recordings of the work in the form of compact discs, cassettes or video tapes. Generally, "reproduction" also includes transmission in digital form of materials on the Internet but temporary transmission in the course of processing in computers is exempted from the right of reproduction.

- *Right to issue copies of works* to the public by sale, lease or lending. This right allows the copyright holder to prevent the distribution of unauthorised copies of a work. In addition, the right allows the copyright holder to control the first distribution of a particular authorised copy. However, the distribution right is limited by the "first sale doctrine", which states that after the first sale or distribution of a copy, the copyright holder can no longer control what happens to that copy. Thus, after a book has been purchased at a book store (the first sale of a copy), the copyright holder has no say over how that copy is further distributed. Thus, the book could be rented or resold without the permission of the copyright holder.

- *Right of public performance* allows the copyright holder to control the public performance of certain copyrighted works. Public performance right is limited to literary works, musical works, dramatic works, choreographic works, pantomimes, motion pictures, and audio visual works. Under the public performance right, rights holders are allowed to control when the work is performed "publicly". A performance is considered "public" when the work is performed in a "place open to the public or at a place where a substantial number of persons outside of a normal circle of a family and its social acquaintances are gathered". A performance is also considered to be public if it is transmitted to multiple locations, such as through television and radio in a pub. It would be a violation of the public performance right in a film to rent a video and to show it in a public park or theatre without obtaining a licence from the copyright holder. In contrast, the performance of the video on a home TV where friends and family are gathered would not be considered a "public" performance and would not be prohibited under the CDPA.

- *Right of making adaptation* allows right holders to transform a pre-existing work into other forms, such as translation, musical arrangement, dramatisation, fictionalisation, film, sound recording, art reproduction, abridgment, condensation, or any other form in which a work may be recast, transformed or adapted. The work which is adapted is referred to as a "derivative work", which constitutes an independent work the copyright in which is owned by the creator of the derivative work, although the permission of the author of the original work is required for the adaptation. In the computer industry, a second version of a software program (for instance Microsoft Office 2007) is generally considered a derivative work based upon the earlier version (such as Office 2000).

- *Right of communication to the public*, including the right of broadcasting and the right of making available to the public. For the former, it allows the right holder to control the broadcast by radio, television, cable or satellite. Making available to the public, on the other hand, referred to the right to control "on-demand delivery" to members of the public from a place and at a time individually chosen by them, for instance downloading or uploading works over the Internet.

MORAL RIGHTS

In addition to exclusive rights which afford economic gains to right holders, CDPA 1988 also provides moral rights to authors who are concerned about their moral merits in relation to dignity, reputation and autonomy. There are a number of rights granted within the CDPA that are personal to the author, as follows:

- *Paternity right*: is the right of the creator to be identified whenever the work is published, exhibited or broadcast etc. This right has to be asserted in any agreement or licence in order to be operative.
- *Right of integrity*: protects the creator from "derogatory treatment" of the work, legally defined as any addition to, deletion from, alteration to or adaptation from the work which amounts to a distortion or mutilation of the work or is otherwise prejudicial to the honour or reputation of the author. However, this does not relate to criticism or where a criminal offence such as obscenity or defamation may result.
- *Right to object to false attribution*: is the right of a person not to be attributed as the author of a work which is created by someone else, therefore protecting one's reputation.
- *Right of privacy*: is different from other moral rights in that a commissioner of a work for private purposes may require that the work is not circulated to the public, for instance by exhibition or broadcast.

Moral rights cannot be assigned but can be waived. There are some exceptions to moral rights as well, mainly relating to the reporting of current events and entries in dictionaries, encyclopaedias etc.

OWNERSHIP OF COPYRIGHT

The author of a copyright work is generally the person who creates it. In relation to sound recordings this is the producer. In films, the principal director and producer are joint authors. The author of a broadcast is the producer who makes and delivers it, ie the broadcaster. The publisher of

a typographical arrangement of a published edition is the author. Where
two or more people collaborate in creating a work and their individual
contributions are not distinct, they are joint authors of that work. Where
two or more persons collaborate but it is possible to determine the separate
parts attributable to each author, it will not be a work of joint authorship
and each person is the author of his own part.

The first owner of the copyright, in most cases, is the author or maker
of the copyright material. Copyright can be assigned by the author to
another party. There may be more than one copyright owner, for example
in co-authored books or journal articles. There may also be more than one
copyright owner in films, where the soundtrack, music, screenplay and the
film as a whole all have separate copyrights.

If the work was created as part of a person's employment then copyright
is generally owned by the employer, eg copyright in material created
by professional staff at a newspaper is owned by the newspaper, if there
is no contrary contractual arrangement. Academic staff at a university
would own copyright in any scholarly works that they create during
spare time but the university owns copyright in any teaching material
created by academic staff in the course of their employment. If a work is
commissioned, the copyright owner will be determined by an agreement
between the creator and the person commissioning the work. Without an
agreement, the author is considered the copyright owner.

It is important to distinguish between ownership of a physical product
and ownership of the copyright embodied within it. Copyright ownership
is different to physical ownership of a work. Just physically owning an
item does not mean owning the copyright in the item. This is particularly
important for original artworks and photographs. For example, the
purchase of a CD does not mean that the purchaser owns the copyright
in the musical or literary work within it or the copyright in the sound
recording. Therefore purchasing a CD alone does not entitle the purchaser
to copy the work or do any other acts which are restricted to the copyright
owner. Unless an agreement is made with the artist, or creator of the
work, for the transfer of copyright ownership, there is no ownership of
copyright. The artist will still have the right to reproduce, publish or
communicate the artwork that a purchaser owns. There are also special
provisions for photographs.

MULTIPLE COPYRIGHT

A work can often have several copyright holders with an interest in it. In a
sound recording the composer of the music has copyright in the music but

the producer has copyright in the recording. If another music company intends to reproduce the sound recording, it needs to ask for permission from both the composer and the producer of the sound recording and to pay remuneration subject to contract. A work can also be jointly owned, where the copyright is enjoyed by two or more persons but can be divided into specific parts, each of which is owned by one author.

DURATION OF COPYRIGHT

Copyright in original musical, literary, dramatic and artistic works lasts until 70 years after the death of the author. The copyright in films also lasts for 70 years after the death of the last to survive of the principal director, the author of the screenplay and dialogue and the composer of the music created specifically for the film. Copyright protection in sound recordings and broadcasts exists for 50 years from the end of the calendar year in which it was made or released. Copyright in the typographical arrangement of published editions exists for 25 years from first publication.

Where the work has originated from outside the European Community or the author is not an EC national, the situation is slightly different. In this case the copyright will generally last for as long as the work attracts copyright protection in the country of origin (usually the country where the work is first published) or, if unpublished, the author's national country, as long as that period does not exceed the period for which UK copyright law protects works of EC origin.

EXPLOITATION OF COPYRIGHT

Copyright owners can exploit their copyright in a number of ways which can be linked to financial or other benefits that will apply to the work in perpetuity or will have restrictions on the scope of the licence granted. A transfer of copyright is usually either an assignment or a licence. An assignment of copyright is operated in the same way as in the sale of personal property. The original owner sells its rights to another party, and can no longer exercise control over how the third party uses those rights. Another way of exploiting copyright is by issuing a licence, which is an agreement where the copyright owner maintains its ownership of the rights involved, but allows a third party to exercise some or all of those rights without fear of a copyright infringement suit. A licence will be preferred over an assignment of rights where the copyright holder wishes to maintain some ownership over the rights, or wishes to exercise continuing control over how the third party uses the copyright holder's rights.

Assignment

Copyright is a property right and therefore like physical property it can be assigned. An assignment is the permanent transfer of copyright from one person (initially the creator) to another. Assignment also takes place by will, in the same way as any other personal property. This essentially removes all interest in and influence over the work from the creator and so should only be done when there are clear benefits. It is possible to sell either certain exclusive rights while retaining others, or all exclusive rights. For instance an author of a book can sell the right of reproduction to a publisher but keep all other exclusive rights. Where another publisher intends to reproduce the book they need to ask for permission from the original publisher. However, where a film producer intends to adapt the book into a film he must ask for permission from the author of the book who retains the right of adaptation. To be valid, any assignment of copyright must be made in writing and signed by or on behalf of the copyright owner.

Future assignment

The CDPA 1988 allows a copyright owner to agree to assign the copyright in works that he will create in the future. When such works come into existence they will automatically transfer to the assignee in the agreement. The ability to assign copyright in future works is particularly useful in relation to authors who are members of a collecting society, so that they can sell their rights separately and individually in the way of future assignment other than the dealing of their existing copyright made by collecting societies on their behalf.

Licences

A licence is a contract between two or more parties that sets out the terms of the agreement. There are three main types of licence for copyright contracts.

- **Exclusive licences** grant sole reproduction right to one legal entity, for specific purposes and/or in defined geographical locations. This also has the effect of excluding all others, including the copyright holder, from exploiting the works for those purposes for the duration of the licence. Such agreements must be made in writing.
- **Non-exclusive licences** do not give sole reproduction rights but simply permit someone to use the copyrighted work for defined purposes. Several similar agreements could be in place at one time even for precisely similar arrangements.

- **Blanket licences** are contracts for use of copyrighted material but are issued by a licensing body for use across a defined copyrighted material user group. The most well-defined scheme is that operated by the Copyright Licensing Agency that confers permission on staff and students at academic institutions to use copyright material under certain well-defined limits.

Compulsory licences

Compulsory licence is the permission granted by the Copyright Tribunal for third parties to access copyright works for the purposes of productive or transformative use without the consent of the owner and upon payment of a stipulated fee. It facilitates transactions in the absence of the owner's consent, usually involving setting the fees for compulsory licensing below the market rate for access to any given copyright work. There are a number of instances where the Secretary of State can grant licences pursuant to statute. These include rental right and reprographic licences for educational institutions. The Secretary of State can make an order providing that, in specified cases, lending copies of artistic, dramatic, literary or musical works, sound recordings or films shall be treated as licensed by the copyright owner subject only to the payment of such reasonable royalty or other payment as may be agreed or determined in default of agreement by the Copyright Tribunal. An application to settle such royalty or other sum payable may be made by the copyright owner or the person claiming to be treated as licensed.

MONITORING COPYRIGHT

Once a work has copyright established, the holder needs to make sure that it is exploited in the most advantageous aesthetic and economic ways. Licensing of copyright can be undertaken and administered in different ways:

- the owner can be responsible for their own works;
- publishers of works can act on the owner's behalf;
- collecting societies can act on behalf of members who own copyright.

Modern technology can make tracing use or misuse of works extremely difficult. It can be equally difficult for potential users of copyrighted material to find out where permission can be obtained. There are a number of well-established mechanisms that have been developed over the years that provide the ways for the copyright holder to exploit their intellectual property, mainly through collecting societies.

Copyright collecting societies

A copyright collecting society, either as the owner or the prospective owner of copyright or as an agent for him, negotiates or grants copyright licences, collects royalties from users and distributes revenues to members. Its licences usually cover the works of more than one author. A copyright collecting society provides a simple method of gaining authorisation to copy, removing the need to seek permission from a right holder on an individual basis each time. It does what an individual creator cannot do for himself. As such, one of the underlying concepts of copyright collecting societies is to save on transaction costs of copyright administration. In practice, within any sector there is more than one collecting society from which authors can choose the most competitive one. Major collecting societies are as following:

- Artists' Collecting Society (ACS);
- Authors' Licensing & Collecting Society (ALCS);
- British Equity Collecting Society (BECS);
- Broadcasting Data Services (BDS);
- Copyright Licensing Agency (CLA);
- Design and Artists Copyright Society (DACS);
- Directors UK (D-UK);
- Educational Recording Agency (ERA);
- Mechanical-Copyright Protection Society (MCPS);
- Motion Picture Licensing Company (MPLC);
- Newspaper Licensing Agency (NLA);
- Open University Worldwide (OUW);
- Performing Right Society (PRS);
- Phonographic Performance Limited (PPL);
- Publishers' Licensing Society (PLS);
- Video Performance Limited (VPL).

INFRINGEMENT OF COPYRIGHT

The copyright holder has a legal right to prevent infringements of his copyright which fall into two main categories:

- **Primary infringement** takes place where a person undertakes a "restricted act" by copying, performing, broadcasting or in any other way using a work without the express permission of the copyright holder.

- **Secondary infringement** takes place where a person knowingly uses, possesses, deals in, imports or exports illegal copies of copyrighted material.

Primary infringers may be liable even if they are not aware they are infringing copyright. To make a claim for copyright infringement, the copyright owner must prove that the infringement is "substantial". To determine whether the unauthorised use of a work is substantial, the courts first identify the work for the purposes of infringement and secondly examine whether the substantial part of the work was used. It should be noted that "substantiality" refers to "quality" rather than "quantity". In the case of copyright infringement, copyright law provides both civil and criminal liabilities and look at whether any profits have been generated from the utilisation of the copyright work. A number of remedies are provided:

- interdicts/injunctions that can be used to prevent further use of the materials;
- damages according to the loss of earnings or royalties to the holder;
- destruction of any materials that are produced in breach of copyright.

The above penalties are available for the breach of moral rights but an interdict/injunction is only available in cases of the breach of right of integrity.

DEFENCES TO COPYRIGHT INFRINGEMENT

Fair dealing

The fair dealing defence was one of the common defences by which the rights enforceable under copyright could be overridden in certain situations. The courts have long held that, as long as any infringement was fairly done, for the benefit of the public, a man might fairly adopt part of the work of another. The Copyright Act 1911 (UK) incorporated the first statutory fair dealing defence and it has been retained in the subsequent copyright legislation, including CDPA, based on a recognition that the public interest demands that not every unauthorised reproduction of copyright material should constitute an infringement of copyright. A number of exceptions to copyright are allowed.

- *Research and private study*: fair dealing of a work for the purpose of non-commercial research or private study does not infringe copyright in the work. The defence applies where the dealing takes place with literary, dramatic, musical, and artistic works, as well as with the typographical formats of a published work. The exception does not apply where the dealing is with a broadcast, sound recording or film. The defence is also limited in relation to computer programs. "Research" means research under any circumstances including commercial research and "private study" means study outside of academic institutions. Only a single copy may be made and separate rules govern sound and broadcast media.

- *Criticism and review*: this covers copying works for the purpose of critical study or review of work for journalistic or academic purposes. There are limits on the length of extracts that can be used. Sufficient acknowledgment of the source is usually needed when critiquing someone's work.

- *Reporting of current events*: fair dealing with any work (other than a photograph) for the purpose of reporting current events does not infringe the copyright in the work, provided that it is accompanied by a sufficient acknowledgment. No acknowledgment of the reporting by means of a sound recording, film, or broadcast is required where this would be impossible by reason of practicality or otherwise. The important word to note in this exception, however, is the term "current". For this exception to apply, the event to which the copyright work pertains must be current and the exception will not apply if the reporting is grossly retrospective.

There is a two-stage test in order for a fair dealing defence to succeed: first, the defendant must show that the use of the copyright work was for one of the stated purposes and, secondly, it must be shown that the use of the work was fair. There is no definition in the CDPA of what will constitute a "fair" dealing but it is well established that this is a question of degree. In *Pro Sieben Media AG* v *Carlton UK Television* (1999), Pro Sieben owned the copyright of a broadcast programme featuring an interview with A, who was carrying eight live embryos after having fertility treatment. The interview was due to be shown on German television. However, Carlton showed an extract from the interview as part of a programme on "chequebook journalism", a programme about current events. It included a 30-second slice of video taken from a full television programme, where substantial fees had been paid for the interview. The Court of Appeal held that the inclusion of the quotation was fair dealing and the question was one of degree or of fact and impression. Further, the interview taken from Pro Sieben was not the only piece of work used, as many pieces of work were also criticised in Carlton's programme. Therefore they did not put up unfair competition for Pro Sieben. The court also held that Carlton's programme contained an acknowledgment in the form of the television company's logo shown in the clip, which was sufficient acknowledgment. Carlton also complied with s 30(2) of the CDPA, as A's pregnancy was a current event.

In *Hyde Park Residence Ltd* v *Yelland* (2000), the *Sun* newspaper published an article entitled "Video that Shames Fayed" along with three video stills which showed Diana, Princess of Wales, and Dodi Al Fayed arriving at and departing from the Villa Windsor in Paris. These still pictures were taken from a security camera owned by the plaintiff company, Hyde Park Residences Ltd, and were sold by an employee of the security firm, Mr Murrell, to the newspaper for a substantial sum of money. Hyde Park Residences Ltd brought summary judgment proceedings on the ground of infringement of its copyright in the stills. The *Sun* claimed that it published the stills in order to discredit statements made by Mohamed Al Fayed concerning the time Princess Diana and Dodi Al Fayed spent at the property and argued that the publication was within the ambit of fair dealing. The court held that there was no fair dealing because the purpose of the newspaper's use was not reporting current events, and that, in any case, the dealing was not fair, given the fact that the work was unpublished and that the information could have been communicated without publishing the stills. The court concluded that the claim for the defence "was an attempt to dress up the infringement of Hyde Park's copyright in the guise of reporting current events" and that to allow the defence would "give honour to dishonour".

It should be noted that it is criticism or review of the content, not the subject of the work, that can be allowed as fair dealing. In *Ashdown* v *Telegraph Group Ltd* (2001), Ashdown, a past Liberal Democratic Party Leader, prepared minutes of a meeting between him and some senior Labour Party members in October 1997 when they had discussed the possibility of co-operation between Labour and the Liberal Democrats. The *Telegraph* published an extract of the minutes, leading to Ashdown bringing an action against the *Telegraph* for violation of copyright. The *Telegraph* sought to rely on the defence that the reproduction was "fair dealing for the purposes of criticism or review" but the claim was rejected by the court on the ground that the work itself was not the object of its criticism. The Court of Appeal further held that a defence of "fair dealing for the purpose of reporting current events" was arguable, saying that a liberal interpretation should be given to the provision, which was "intended to protect the role of the media in informing the public about matters of current concern to the public". By implication, therefore, matters could be historical but of current concern and thus within the ambit of the defence. But that did not apply in this case, having regard especially to the quantity of the work taken.

Disclosure in the public interest

This defence would usually apply to, for example, documents which relate to a pressing public affair which must be disclosed regardless of its copyright protection. The "public interest defence" does not deny copyright protection to a work; it merely prevents the claimant from enforcing its copyright against the defendant. Although this defence was recognised by the High Court in the 1970s and the Court of Appeal in the 1980s, it was controversial and has been debated by both courts and commentators over the last few years. The recent decisions, for instance *Hyde Park Residence Ltd* v *Yelland* (2000), offer little assistance as to when the public interest defence would apply, except to indicate that the circumstances are more limited than in cases of breach of confidence. The court rejected the public interest defence on the ground that s 171(3) of the CDPA "does not give the court a general power to enable an infringer to use another's property, namely his copyright, in the public interest". It stated that copyright is a property right which is given by the 1988 Act and it would be wrong for a court, having rejected a fair dealing defence, to uphold a defence because publication was in the public interest. It further considered that "copyright is concerned with the protection of the form of the works in which copyright can subsist and not the protection of information". Therefore, given that public interest was recognised for breach of confidence, it was unnecessary for the copyright issue. The court was also of the view that "accepting a general defence of public interest would appear to be contrary to [England's] international obligations".

In contrast, in *Ashdown* v *Telegraph Group Ltd* (2001), the court noted that the possibility of a public interest defence was already recognised under the Copyright Act. However, it held that the circumstances in which public interest may override copyright are very rare and "are not capable of precise categorisation or definition". Nonetheless it rejected the *Telegraph*'s claim for public interest. It held that the *Telegraph* could have made limited quotation of the actual words, to demonstrate that it had obtained the actual minutes, and was in a position to give an authentic account. But that was not what it had done. Generally, if a newspaper makes unauthorised use of the work of another, it should have to pay compensation or account for the profits made unless it can bring its actions within one of the prescribed limitations or exceptions to the CDPA.

Incidental inclusion

Copyright in a work is not infringed by its "incidental inclusion" in an artistic work, sound recording, film, or broadcast. This means that there is no liability where a copyright work, such as a painting, is incidentally included in the background of another work, such as a film. Section 32(2) of the CDPA includes the exploitation of works that incidentally include other works. The showing of a film, as a result, does not infringe.

Educational uses

In addition to the fair dealing defences, the CDPA contains a number of defences that relate to copying carried out by schools and other educational establishments including universities and colleges of further education. The defences include copying for instruction and examination; copying short passages in anthologies and collections; performing, playing or showing works; recording of broadcasts; reprographic copying; and lending of copies.

Essential Facts

- The subject-matter of copyright includes literary works, artistic works, dramatic works, musical works, films, sound recordings, broadcasts and typographic arrangements.
- Exclusive rights cover the right to copy, the right to issue copies to the public, the right of public performance, the right of adaptation and the right of communication to the public.
- Moral rights include paternity right, the right of integrity and the right to object to false attribution. Privacy right is associated with moral rights.

- A number of defences to copyright infringement are available, eg fair dealing including research and private study, criticism and review and reporting of current events, public interest, incidental inclusion and educational use etc.

Essential Cases

Pro Sieben Media AG v Carlton UK Television (1999): the court held that fair dealing is a question of degree as to whether the use of materials competes with the exploitation of copyright by the copyright owner. The court also examined the requirement for sufficient acknowledgment.

Hyde Park Residence Ltd v Yelland (2000): the court rejected the existence of a public interest defence under the CDPA.

Ashdown v Telegraph Group Ltd (2001): the court rejected the *Telegraph*'s claim for fair dealing, holding that in fair dealing the object of criticism must be the content of the work. The court also recognised the public interest defence under the CDPA but it held that the circumstances in which public interest may override copyright are very rare and difficult to define.

10 UK MEDIA REGULATION

The traditional mass media comprise two sectors: the print media and the electronic media, ie radio and television broadcasting. As they have different historical origins, these two distinctive sectors of the media have been subject to different regulatory measures. Following an industrial model, the Press is subject to minimum regulation and has developed in a highly competitive market, in particular in the area of local newspapers. Therefore the print media are entirely self-regulating in the United Kingdom and operate free of any specific statutory rules. The profession has established the Press Complaints Commission on its own initiative, and this body has developed a code of practice against which to measure journalistic standards. On the other hand, the broadcast media are subject to a number of specific rules. Apart from these self-regulation and statutory regulation, all media are subject to general laws, such as those relating to defamation, obscenity and hate speech.

By contrast, broadcasting has been heavily regulated since its birth, when it was growing out of a need to establish a public monopoly of broadcasting which excluded competition. In 1922 the British Broadcasting Company was granted a licence as a sole radio broadcaster, and was reshaped later in 1927 to become the British Broadcasting Corporation (BBC). Its monopoly status in radio persisted till the 1970s and in television until the mid-1950s when commercial television was introduced.

The economic and political changes after the Second World War led broadcasting into a new landscape where the BBC's monopoly on television was broken by the introduction of the first commercial television channel in 1954, whereby the public/commercial paradigm of broadcasting structure was established. With the growth of the advertising and programmes industries, the economic importance of broadcasting received recognition and private companies expressed enthusiasm for exploiting the commercial potentials of broadcasting. Amid requests from both private capital and the general public for more channels, the break-up of the public monopoly received support from the then ruling Conservative Party and consequently a Broadcasting Act was passed in 1954, whereby the door of broadcasting was opened to commercial companies and the first commercial channel ITV was set up. The programme markets in both supply and consumption have greatly expanded and this gave rise to the introduction of more delivery channels, including Channel 4 and Channel 5. With the expansion of the broadcasting industry as a result of advancements in communications technology, a number of pieces of broadcasting legislation have been introduced, most prominently the Broadcasting Acts 1990 and 1996. The Communications Act 2003 is the most recently updated broadcasting legislation which accommodates the requirements of communications convergence. These pieces of legislation set out broad categories of material which should be covered by codes of conduct but leave detailed elaboration of these categories to regulatory bodies to monitor and apply the codes.

Among these codes of practice, Ofcom's Broadcasting Code and the Press Complaints Commission's Code of Practice are the most prominent ones that provide guidance for broadcasters and the press media with regard to content standards, varying from good taste, decency, impartiality, crime, religion, privacy and information gathering, fairness and the reporting of elections and referenda, to right to reply. It should be noted that these standards, although covering the major subject-matters of journalistic reporting, tend to be principled because of the complexity of the world and leave much discretional power to Ofcom and the PCC to interpret in their adjudication of individual cases.

The objectives of media regulation cover a variable range. From the political perspective, maintenance of a diversity of media output is considered vital to a democracy; in an economic sense, prevention and control of media monopoly serve to promote a competitive economy which benefits both the industry and consumers; a social concern can be discerned from, for instance, universal service provision which is aimed at making the media universally available to citizens. Although derived from different perspectives, these regulatory concerns are by no means isolated but interrelated, competing as well as overlapping. Therefore there is always an issue of priority to be given, to the political end or economic objectives. The interrelation of these concerns can be seen in that not only could economic benefits advance social development but also economic and social objectives must be established on the basis of a democratic foundation.

SELF-REGULATION OF THE PRESS BY THE PRESS COMPLAINTS COMMISSION

In the United Kingdom, the print media are essentially subject to self-regulation. There is no statutory body to regulate the Press and no requirement for journalists to be registered or be affiliated with any particular institution. The Press is mainly regulated by a body established by newspapers themselves: the Press Complaints Commission.

The Press Complaints Commission (PCC) was established in response to the widespread complaints of the general public against the aggressive intrusion of newspapers and magazines into individuals' privacy and other personal arenas, following a public inquiry which proposed, with a threat to set up a statutory Press Council if no improvement were made, the establishment of a voluntary body to regulate the Press to improve ethical journalism standards.

The PCC draw up a Code of Practice and the practitioners, editors and journalists committed to be subject to the code. The PCC is funded by a levy on newspapers and periodicals and it was agreed that a majority of those on the PCC would be lay people. The main purposes of the PCC were to set high standards for journalism, to disseminate and promote those standards, to provide training for journalists, to receive complaints against newspapers and magazines and adjudicate on them, and generally to maintain the highest standards of journalism in the British Press. Membership of the PCC is essentially voluntary, although in practice all major newspapers are members.

Once established, the PCC started dealing with complaints and issuing guidelines, which are kept updated frequently. Since the Code of Practice was introduced there have been a number of revisions in its structure and content. The revision of the Code is undertaken by the Code of Practice Committee, which comprises senior editors from the newspaper and magazine industry.

The current Code of Practice covers a wide range of issues, from accuracy, intrusion and right of reply to discrimination. Among them, seven articles, including privacy, harassment, children, payment to criminals and reporting of crimes, are subject to a "public interest test" which, by taking into account the circumstances, overrides the rules if the public interest is at stake. As no clear definition of "public interest" is stated in the Code, the application of the public interest override gives the PCC significant discretion when interpreting the Code and there is no shortage of controversy and criticism about the PCC's adjudication.

The PCC has proven a cost-effective mechanism. Any member of the public can make a complaint to the PCC, claiming breach by a newspaper or magazine of the Code. There is no charge for making complaints and no legal representation is required. The PCC requires that most complaints should be dealt with quickly. The complaint procedure is governed by a "complainants' charter" against which satisfaction of complainants can be measured. However, the remedies are limited under the PCC, with the only "sanction" for breach of the Code being a requirement that the offending newspaper publish the findings of the PCC. In the past, a number of newspapers withdrew from the PCC in protest about its findings, yet these newspapers later rejoined the PCC.

BROADCASTING REGULATION UNDER OFCOM

Unlike the Press, broadcasting regulation in the UK is based on statute and is relatively complex. Commercial television and radio are regulated by the Office of Communications (Ofcom). The Communications Act 2003 requires Ofcom to establish certain codes to which licensees must conform; the major one is the Broadcasting Code. Ofcom also has broad powers to sanction broadcasters who breach licence conditions, such as fines, suspension or even revocation of licences. The British Broadcasting Corporation (BBC), a public service broadcaster, is not subject to Ofcom licensing, and has instead established an internal system to deal with complaints. All broadcasters – public and private, radio and television – are subject to Ofcom's Broadcasting Code.

Ofcom is the product of a merger among five former regulatory bodies, namely the telecommunications regulator (Oftel), the television and radio regulators (Independent Television Commission and Radio Authority), a government agency responsible for spectrum licensing (Radio Communications Agency) and a regulator with distinct responsibility for standards and fairness in broadcasting (Broadcasting Standards Commission). Ofcom is also responsible for implementing EU regulations on electronic communications (as discussed in Chapter 11). It also inherited from Oftel the competition law powers over communications businesses.

In the Communications Act 2003, Ofcom is expressly required to "further the interests of the persons who are customers" for regulated services and facilities, and to "promote competition". Balancing these duties is a matter for Ofcom's discretion. Its principal duties are "to further the interests of citizens in relation to communications matters", and "to further the interests of customers in relevant markets, where appropriate by promoting competition". However, Ofcom's practice in keeping a balance between these interests has been controversial, for instance in its decision requiring BSkyB to cut by 23 per cent the price that it charges rivals for its sports programmes.

Ofcom's duties are split into content functions and network functions, which are performed in different ways. Under Ofcom, the Content Board is responsible for television and radio content regulation, including, to a limited extent, regulation of the BBC's output. With regard to network functions in relation to competition issues, Ofcom has concurrent powers with the Office of Fair Trading to apply the Competition Act in relation to the communications sector, and has the added function of applying the Competition Act in relation to media mergers.

Under the Communications Act 2003, Ofcom's licensees are obliged to obey the provisions of its codes, including advertising, programme standards, fairness, privacy and sponsorship. Ofcom deals with complaints from the public relating to programme content and can also take action of its own accord. Complainants can contact the broadcaster in the first instance or otherwise make complaints directly to Ofcom. Complaints should be made within a reasonable time, as broadcasters are required to keep recordings for only the following periods of time: radio, 42 days; television, 90 days; and cable and satellite, 60 days. Ofcom may advise, warn or fine broadcasters and, in extreme cases, may shorten, suspend or revoke a broadcasting licence. All action taken by Ofcom is post-broadcast. It does not review material before it is broadcast, although it may provide guidance to producers if requested.

LICENSING OF BROADCASTING

Under the Communications Act 2003, Ofcom is responsible for licensing and regulating the TV services provided by ITV, Channel 4, Channel 5, cable operators, BSkyB, and other providers of TV services via any of satellite, cable or DTT for reception in the UK, such as Flextech, Viacom and Discovery. The BBC is not regulated by Ofcom but by its own Charter; and S4C, the Welsh fourth channel, is a separate statutory authority funded by the Government.

The Communications Act classifies some persons as disqualified persons who are not permitted to hold TV licences. Disqualified persons include any bodies whose objects are wholly or mainly of a political or religious nature and advertising agencies. The Communications Act also provides for a person to be disqualified if it is owned more than 5 per cent by a disqualified person or if it is otherwise associated with a disqualified person in any manner specified in the relevant provisions of the 2003 Act.

Terrestrial television licences

The ITV (Independent Television) network was set up on a regional basis in 1955 to provide competition for the BBC. It comprised a number of independent franchised licensees, the majority of which have now merged to form ITV plc. The network generates funds through broadcasting television advertisements. Its flagship analogue channel was renamed "ITV1" in 2001 as part of a rebranding exercise to coincide with the creation of a number of digital-only channels. These now include ITV2, ITV3, ITV4, ITV Play and CiTV. ITV Network Centre is wholly owned by the ITV companies and undertakes commissioning and scheduling of programmes shown across the ITV network and, as with the other terrestrial channels, 25 per cent of its programmes must come from independent producers.

Channel 4 and S4C were launched in 1982 to provide programmes with a distinctive character that appeal to interests not catered for by ITV. Although publicly owned, Channel 4 receives no public funding and is financed by commercial activities, including advertising. S4C's digital service, S4C Digital, broadcasts entirely in the Welsh language. Channel 4 has expanded to create the digital stations E4, More4 and Film4.

Channel 5 (later renamed Five) began broadcasting in 1997. Despite initial problems with limited coverage, it now reaches about 80 per cent of the population. Digital stations Five US and Five Life (later renamed Fiver) were launched in October 2006.

Satellite television services licences

The broadcasting services provided by BSkyB are provided under satellite television services (STS) licences issued by Ofcom. Under EC law, satellite broadcasters which have their principal place of business in the UK are regulated by UK authorities. An STS licence permits the operation of an STS service but does not confer on an STS licensee the right to use any specific satellite, transponder or frequency to deliver the service. It relates to the provision of the service, not the network via which such service is delivered. STS licences are granted for a period of 10 years and new licences are issued by Ofcom if certain minimum objective criteria are met. Ofcom has authority to impose fines, shorten the licence period or revoke licences if, *inter alia*, the licensee breaches or fails to remedy a breach of any licence condition or to comply with any direction which Ofcom lawfully gives to the STS licensee. In addition, Ofcom may revoke a licence in order to enforce the restrictions contained in the Communications Act 2003 on the ownership of media companies. Ofcom has wide discretion to vary the conditions of licences issued under the Communications Act.

Digital terrestrial television licences

The Communications Act 2003 enhances the framework for the development of digital terrestrial broadcasting, involving the licensing of multiplex operators, digital programme service (DPS) providers and digital additional service providers. A multiplex is a frequency band on which several programme services can be combined.

Six TV multiplexes are currently available. In addition to the multiplex granted to BSkyB, in June 2002, following the collapse of ITV Digital, the digital terrestrial television licence was awarded to a consortium made up of the BBC, BSkyB and the transmitter company Crown Castle by the Independent Television Commission. Freeview, a new digital network, was launched on 30 October 2002. Freeview offers around 30 digital channels and requires the purchase of a set-top box, but is subsequently free of charge.

MEDIA OWNERSHIP RULES

The Act provides for ownership provisions affecting the broadcasting industry. The aim of ownership rules is to promote competition and investment, while the public interest and media plurality are balanced through a "plurality test" (as discussed below), public service broadcasting obligations and the continuance of some ownership restrictions.

- **Foreign ownership**: the removal of foreign (non-EU) ownership restrictions applying to the analogue broadcast licences of ITV, Channel 5 and all local and national AM and FM radio stations (digital stations are excluded from this rule).
- **Cross-media ownership**: this allows a national newspaper group to purchase Channel 5, subject to the plurality test. National newspaper groups with a 20 per cent or more national market share are still prevented from buying ITV. A parallel rule limits local newspapers with a 20 per cent or more local market share from owning the overlapping ITV service.
- **Ownership rule for radios**: its objective is to "ensure a plurality of sources of news and information by ensuring that in every area where there is a reasonable range of services (in practice, three or more), there will be at least two local radio operators, in addition to the BBC".
- **National newspapers' ownership of ITV**: a business with a national newspaper market share of 20 per cent or more will continue to be prohibited from holding an interest of more than 20 per cent in an

ITV company, which, for instance, precludes News Corporation from buying into the key mass market commercial broadcaster.

- **Local newspaper/ITV rule**: this will stop a business with a local newspaper market share of 20 per cent or more from controlling the ITV company covering that area, so that a local newspaper group such as Johnston Press or Scotsman Publications would be restricted from participating in ITV.

- **Local cross-media ownership**: this is a potential obstacle to merger activity in relation to radio groups. It sets a lower 45 per cent maximum points threshold if the merger partner holds 50 per cent or more of the relevant local newspaper market, or holds an ITV licence covering more than 50 per cent of the radio station's potential audience. Ownership of a local radio station will be prohibited if the acquiror holds both 50 per cent or more of the relevant local newspaper market and such an ITV licence.

- **Miscellaneous ownership**: there has been a relaxation of various other media ownership restrictions. Broadcasters can now hold up to 40 per cent (up from 20 per cent) of ITN. Advertising agencies may now purchase UK television and radio broadcasters. Prohibitions on religious organisations controlling broadcast licences have been relaxed to a limited extent and local authorities can now own broadcast licences for specific purposes.

Section 391 of the Act requires Ofcom to review the media ownership rules at least every 3 years and make recommendations to the Secretary of State if changes to the rules are needed.

THE PLURALITY TEST FOR MEDIA MERGERS

The Communications Act 2003 replaces the previous special regime for mergers between newspaper groups, under which certain such mergers required prior consent by the Secretary of State for Trade and Industry after a compulsory Competition Commission inquiry. The Act applies the general merger control rules under the Enterprise Act 2002 to mergers involving newspapers where no public interest issue is concerned.

Where a newspaper merger gives rise to concerns about its effects on accurate presentation of news and free expression of opinion in newspapers, Ofcom may assess the merger, applying a plurality test, and report its findings to the Secretary of State.

Following the Ofcom report, these issues may be considered by the Competition Commission (a deal can be referred solely on public interest grounds), and the Secretary of State can order appropriate public interest remedies even if no remedies are necessary from a competition perspective. This is consistent with the general Enterprise Act framework, which applies similar special rules to mergers involving public interest considerations.

A similar plurality test applies to a broadcaster merger that has negative effects on pluralism. Both Ofcom and the Competition Commission may recommend that the Secretary of State order remedies. The issues which Ofcom and the Competition Commission will assess are the merger's effects on the plurality of persons with control of media enterprises, the need for availability of a wide range of high quality and diverse broadcasting, and the need for maintenance of standards in television or radio. The Secretary of State may make a public interest intervention, but is not obliged to do so, which implies it is a discretional political decision.

CONTENT REGULATION

The Communications Act 2003 establishes a three-tired framework for content regulation which is more coherent across all broadcasters and relies more on self-regulation. The first tier covers basic requirements: standards of programme content for TV and radio and compliance with the European Commission's Television Directive. The second tier covers specific requirements that can be measured objectively; production quotas, levels of domestic and international news in peak time, party political broadcasts and schools programmes. Under the third tier the self-regulation is vested in public service broadcasters. Broadcasters are obliged to publish an annual statement of programme policy and to report annually on performance against that statement. Ofcom has jurisdiction over the content regulation conducted by its content board and consumer panel.

Tier One: Broadcasting Code for all broadcasters

Tier One regulation for all radio and television broadcasters (including the BBC, with one exception noted below) is considered as "negative content regulation" about what broadcasters should not do. It is concerned about the content in relation to harm and offence, accuracy and impartiality, fairness and privacy.

To implement the regulation, Ofcom has enacted the Broadcasting Code to ensure that licensees respect their licence conditions with regard to content. The Code prohibits the broadcasting of:

- any programme which impairs the well-being of under-18s;
- material which causes harm and offence;
- matter which incites crime or disorder;
- news which is not impartial and accurate;
- religious programmes which are not responsible; and
- biased reporting of elections and referenda.

The Code provides both general principles and detailed guidance on difficult borderline cases. Broadcasters are required to exercise a great deal of discretion to decide whether or not to broadcast certain types of material. They will need to balance complex competing interests, such as the need to protect children while not overly restricting viewing choices which are suitable for adults. A large number of cases are about the balance between the freedom of expression, ie the right of the public to receive information and ideas from range of sources, and a number of conflicting interest such as privacy, violence in society and impartiality in the news.

Protection of under-18s and harm and offence

This provision requires broadcasters to take necessary measures to protect under-18s and prohibits broadcasting of material that might seriously impair their physical, mental or moral development. Television service providers are also subject to additional obligations under the Audiovisual Media Services Directive regarding protection of children. Children must also be protected by appropriate scheduling from material that is unsuitable for them. There is an assumption that younger audiences generally go to bed earlier so that there is less risk of harm to children from a programme when it is shown late at night than earlier in the evening. Programmes which are unsuitable for children under 18 should not be shown at a time when a significant number of children of that age would be watching television. A "watershed" time is then established whereby material unsuitable for children may not be broadcast before 9 pm or after 5.30 am. Although there is no strict watershed rule for radio, radio broadcasters must have regard to times when children are particularly likely to be listening.

The Code also establishes a provision with regard to harm and offence to ensure that generally accepted standards are applied to television and radio services. This rule restricts broadcasting of harmful and offensive material involving offensive language, violence, sex, sexual violence, humiliation, distress, violation of human dignity, discriminatory treatment or language on the grounds of age, disability, gender, race, religion, beliefs and sexual orientation. Such material is not allowed to be broadcast unless it is justified editorially or by context.

Context includes the following factors:

- the editorial content of the programme, programmes or series;
- the service on which the material is broadcast;
- the time of broadcast;
- other programmes scheduled before and after the programme;
- the degree of harm or offence likely to be caused;
- the potential audience and likely expectation of the audience;
- the nature of the content; and
- the effect of the material on viewers or listeners.

With regard to programmes involving violence, the Code prohibits broadcasting of material which condones or glamorises violence or dangerous or seriously anti-social behaviour and is likely to encourage others to follow such behaviour, in particular methods of suicide and self-harm, unless they are justified editorially and also by context. When a programme portrays exorcism, the occult, the paranormal, divination or practices related to any of these that purport to be real, broadcasters must treat these subjects with due objectivity and make this clear to viewers and listeners. When broadcasting material demonstrating hypnotic techniques, they must take necessary measures to prevent hypnosis or adverse reactions in viewers and listeners, and for instance take precautions to maintain a low level of risk to viewers who have photosensitive epilepsy. Where broadcasters need to broadcast flashing lights, viewers should be given a warning at the start of the programme.

Crime

When depicting crime or anti-social behaviour, broadcasters must strike a balance between accurately portraying real life and the need to avoid inciting or encouraging such behaviour. Broadcasters are not allowed to promise or give payment or payment in kind to convicted or confessed criminals for them to contribute to a programme involving their crime, unless it is justified in the public interest. Criminal or anti-social activities should not be presented as acceptable or in a favourable light, and a programme is not allowed to be broadcast if it could adversely affect the outcome of a criminal investigation.

Religion

When dealing with religion, broadcasters must ensure that the beliefs and practices of the religions depicted are fairly and accurately presented. Those religious views or beliefs of a particular religious group should not be discriminated against. In a programme involving religions the identity of those religions must be clarified. In particular, for non-specialist TV channels religious programmes should not be used to promote religions or seek to recruit.

Privacy and information gathering

As discussed in Chapter 7, Ofcom also deals with privacy issues, providing an appropriate balance between personal privacy, including unnecessary intrusion on the one hand and the public's interest in receiving truthful information and entertainment, even when this might sometimes offend, irritate or intrude upon the privacy of particular individuals.

Due impartiality and due accuracy

The Broadcasting Code provides very detailed guidance on the requirements of impartiality and accuracy in broadcasting, particularly in relation to news and current affairs programming. However, this provision does not apply to the BBC which self-regulates matters according to its own code of practice based on the Royal Charter. The Code aims to ensure that broadcasters present information impartially and accurately and do not use their power to influence public opinion or to favour one viewpoint over another when screening programmes dealing with any of these matters. In contrast, newspaper editors and journalists are not obliged to maintain impartiality on these matters.

This provision requires that news be reported with due accuracy and presented with due impartiality. Where mistakes are made they should be acknowledged and corrected on air in a timely manner. Where a programme covers political policy or industrial controversy, broadcasters need to keep a balance of views without giving undue prominence to any particular view. They may not employ any politician as a newsreader, interviewer or reporter in any news programme unless justified editorially.

"Due impartiality" does not require that every viewpoint be aired in the same manner and for an equal length of time. Instead, the exercise of impartiality can vary according to a number of factors, such as the nature of the subject, the type of programme and channel, and the audience's expectation. Editorial independence must always be strictly observed and no particular viewpoint should be given undue prominence. In particular, broadcasters should not let certain people, including politicians and senior public figures, dictate the topics being covered or the way interviews are presented.

Impartiality in the reporting of elections and referenda

Special rules are put in place under the Communications Act 2003 and also the Broadcasting Code to deal with programmes at election times and referenda, to ensure the impartiality of the news reporting. The code requires that if a candidate takes part in an item about his constituency the broadcaster must ensure that each of the major parties is offered an opportunity to take part. In a radio report of an election in a constituency or electoral area a full list of candidates standing should be given for that constituency. For television, broadcasters should make sure that the lists of candidates for the constituency are available and visible to views for an appropriate period of time. In the programmes broadcasters should give similar opportunities to explore different policy matters within other parties. A broadcaster should include a number of candidates from different parties in one report. Clearly, theses rules seek to prevent discrimination regarding access to broadcasting by any party and no party should benefit from undue prominence in news or other broadcasts.

Fairness

In order to implement the provisions of the Communications Act 2003 and the EC Audiovisual Media Services Directive, the Broadcasting Code provides detailed guidance on issues relating to fairness to ensure that individuals and organisations are equally and fairly treated. In a programme involving individuals the broadcaster should inform participants where they are expected to make contributions to the programme, the nature and purpose of the programme, the types of programme, any significant changes to the programme, and their legal rights in the programme. Where an interviewee is under 16 years old, consent of their parents or guardians must be given and no question beyond the interviewee's capacity to answer should be asked. Before broadcasting factual programmes, broadcasters should check whether the material facts are comprehensive and ensure that no unfair omission of relevant individual or organisations is made. In a programme alleging wrongdoing or incompetence, broadcasters should give those concerned an appropriate and timely opportunity to respond. In general, the Code does not allow broadcasters to obtain information by means of surreptitious filming or recording, unless it is in the public interest and cannot reasonably be obtained by other means. For unsolicited wind-up calls or entertainment set-ups, broadcasters should ask for consent of the individual and organisation concerned before the material is broadcast. For programmes involving celebrities, the Code does not require their consent but if the programme may cause unjustified public ridicule or personal distress to them the use of materials must be justified on the public interest ground.

Tier Two: qualitative requirements

Tier Two regulation concerns the establishment and monitoring of quotas for all public service television broadcasters (ITV, Channel 4, Channel 5 and BBC television) in relation to independent production quotas, regional production quotas, and original (UK/EU) production quotas. Here the aim is to secure a healthy production industry and strong local content.

Tier Three: obligations for public service broadcasters

Tier Three regulation involves monitoring the requirement for commercial public service television broadcasters (ITV, Channel 4 and Channel 5) to meet their public service obligations via an annual system of statements of programme policy.

Under Tier Three regulation, the BBC is required to consider guidance given by Ofcom about the preparation of the BBC's statements on programme policy. The BBC is also required to consider any reports published by Ofcom, such as those produced in the course of the Public Service Television Broadcasting Review.

In radio, there is also a Tier Three equivalent which requires commercial radio stations to adhere to their agreed formats and to the new localness guidance set out in the Communications Act 2003.

THE BRITISH BROADCASTING CORPORATION (BBC)

In 1922 the British Broadcasting Company was granted a Royal Charter to operate as a public service broadcaster and was later reshaped in 1927 to become the British Broadcasting Corporation (BBC). Its licence has a 10-year term and is renewable. The BBC is funded primarily through licence fees, paid by any household or company in the UK that owns a device that can receive television broadcasts. The BBC also sells copyright in its programmes in overseas markets as a supplementary source of funding. The BBC is ruled by the Board of Governors who are drawn from different parts of society and its operation is free from government intervention. Unlike other broadcasters, its obligations are detailed in the agreement between the BBC and the Secretary of State and it is not subject to Ofcom regulation. Both the Royal Charter and the agreement with the executive require the BBC to ensure that its broadcasts are accurate and impartial, do not offend good taste or decency or include anything which is likely to incite or encourage crime, lead to disorder or be offensive to public feeling.

The BBC self-regulates its broadcasts by following its own Editorial Guidelines, dealing with a broad range of matters including impartiality, fairness, privacy, surreptitious recording, taste and decency, violence, conflicts of interest, suffering and distress, children, crime and the police, terrorism and national security, politics and politicians, election broadcasts, and general legal matters such as defamation and contempt.

In general, Ofcom does not have jurisdiction over the BBC but can deal with complaints against the BBC except on issues of impartiality and accuracy. The BBC Complaints Unit also handles complaints at the initial stage. The unit investigates complaints against the standards set out in the Editorial Guidelines and suggests appropriate measures or sanctions where necessary. Where a complainant is unhappy with the decision of the unit he may appeal to the Editorial Complaint Unit.

Essential Facts:

- The Press industry self-regulate the practices of journalists under its Code of Practice. Its decision is not legally binding and is observed voluntarily.
- Radio and television broadcasting is regulated by Ofcom under the Communications Act 2003.
- The 2003 Act sets out restrictive rules on the ownership of the media.
- Broadcasting content is subject to three tiers of regulation.
- The BBC is governed by Royal Charter and its licence is renewable and reviewed once every 10 years.

11 EC MEDIA REGULATION

BACKGROUND

The media regulation in the EC has developed along with the expansion of the EC in both its membership and its jurisdiction. Established in 1957 under the Treaty of Rome, the European Economic Community (EEC, replaced by the EC in 1992) aimed to establish a single market in which persons, goods and services could circulate freely. As a supranational body, the EEC was invested by the Treaty of Rome with the power to act independently in making policies and laws which were to be binding on the Member States.

Originally the media, particularly broadcasting, were subject to national governance when their reach was mainly confined to the territory of a state and there was no explicit provision on broadcasting or reference to the competence of the EC in the Treaty of Rome. Broadcasting was not economically a significant industry when the market was dominated by public service broadcasting (PSB) while commercial broadcasting was under development. Therefore there was no strong impetus for the EC to intervene in domestic broadcasting. However, this did not deny a link between broadcasting and the EC's economic agenda. Where broadcasting was concerned with the Common Market, the EC would step in. In the absence of any explicit provision and reference under the Treaty of Rome with regard to broadcasting, it was the European Court of Justice that, by applying general economic provisions of the Treaty, confirmed jurisdiction of the EC over broadcasting as far as the Common Market was concerned. Later the ECJ further established the EC's jurisdiction to the extent that the EC could change those national regulations which were incompatible with the Common Market doctrine.

The Community's media policy started when commercial television began to flourish in the 1980s as a result of the development of cable and satellite technology. The domestic broadcasting market was becoming attractive to foreign broadcasters with a view to sharing advertising revenues. The fast-developing communications technology greatly increased the economic significance of the media industry in the Common Market. However, national laws, especially with regard to the restrictions on advertising, increasingly became barriers to cable and satellite broadcasting in the Common Market. In view of these potential difficulties, the EC stepped in to harmonise and co-ordinate national laws. However, this was not the only driving force behind the EC's intervention. The cultural significance of broadcasting was also increased when broadcasting became transitional. It was recognised that the dissemination of European programming could help foster European unity and establish European identity against the strong US cultural influence. However, unlike other goods and commodities, broadcasting has not only economic values, but cultural, social and political importance. Foreign programmes had multiple consequences over domestic broadcasting industry, socially, politically and economically. Thus cultural policy was recognised as a domestic matter and the competence of the Community in the media has been controversial ever since.

Against this background, the Television Without Frontiers Directive (TVWF), the Community's first attempt at harmonising domestic laws, was put in place. Member States were required to ensure that all television broadcasts transmitted by broadcasters under their jurisdiction complied with the broadcasting law of that Member State as well as the Directive. It also prohibited Member States from restricting the reception of television broadcasts from other Member States in respect of any matter covered by the Directive. Thus the Directive established an essential principle that guaranteed free transmission and reception of broadcasts within the European Community. To fulfil the mission of broadcasting in promoting cultural diversity, the Directive required European broadcasters to reserve a majority proportion of broadcast time for European works and to allocate at least 10 per cent of their programming budgets for European works created by independent broadcasters. Although the Directive intended to accommodate two concerns – television's economic functions in the Common Market and its role in European cultural construction – the conflict between them was apparent and has remained a theme of the Community's media policy ever since. While the abolition of barriers to transfrontier television received little objection, the quota requirement has remained contested in both theory and practice. With the rapid development of communications technology which brought about communications convergence, the Directive increasingly became inadequate to deal with the issues arising from the new communications environment and was replaced by the Audiovisual Media Services Directive in 2007.

On the other hand, the EC attempted to extend its jurisdiction to the area of media ownership control. Since the 1980s, there has been a tendency towards media concentration and cross-media ownership across the Member States by means of which large companies could take advantage of economies of scale. This brought about the danger of a lack of pluralism since the diversity of information would be potentially limited if the distribution channels were controlled by few owners. Therefore, ownership control was regarded as essential to ensure a diversity of information resources and was put in place in a number of Member States. However, there were significant differences between national regulations which raised concern that the inconsistency of the regulations might obstruct cross-border investment and, consequently, the Common Market. However the uncertainty of the Community's competence in dealing with pluralism issue led to the failure of an attempt to formulate unified EC media ownership rules.

AUDIOVISUAL MEDIA SERVICES DIRECTIVE (AVMS)

In recognition that the TVWF had become outdated, in 2007 the EU adopted the AVMS, incorporated into Member States' domestic law in 2009. The AVMS not only expands the scope of the TVWF but also introduces more detailed rules on television broadcast and new online audiovisual services. The AVMS was introduced in order to:

(a) modernise and simplify the regulatory framework for television broadcasting;

(b) extend the regulatory framework to all forms of "linear" audiovisual media services (ie services which "push" content to viewers, including, for example, all scheduled broadcasting via traditional TV, the Internet or mobile phones); and

(c) introduce harmonised minimum rules for "non-linear" audio-visual media services (ie services which the viewer "pulls" from a network, including, for example, on-demand films or news).

The AVMS was made in the context of the convergence of communications sectors at all levels, including infrastructure, service markets and consumer consumption, whereby broadcasters, newspapers, cable and telecommunications operators could horizontally extend their services to each others' areas on the same platform. The traditional sector-specific regulatory regime under the TVWF could not accommodate the needs of the emerging businesses, causing legal uncertainty and an uneven playing field between new media and traditional media service providers. While new rules are introduced to apply to new services, they do not cover the Internet in order to avoid unnecessary regulatory burdens on this new sector.

Scope of the AVMS

In view of the impact that the new audiovisual media services have on the development of the communications market and consumers' use of new services, the AVMS extends the scope of the TVWF, which covered traditional broadcasts only and left new online services untouched. In particular, under the previous regulatory framework, telecommunications, television and Internet services were each subject to different regulation, causing barriers to entry of the other markets. The broader and more generic definition of audiovisual media services can encompass all communications services, paving the way for communications convergence at a new high level.

Article 1a of the AVMS requires that an audiovisual media service must present simultaneously the following six elements: (1) a "service" within the meaning of the Treaty provisions (Arts 49 and 50 EC); (2) provided under the "editorial responsibility" of a media service provider; (3) the principal purpose of which is the "provision of programmes" consisting of moving images with or without sound; (4) "to inform, entertain or educate"; (5) to the "general public"; (6) by "electronic communications networks". It should be noted that this definition covers only commercial audiovisual media services while excluding personal audiovisual communications on the Internet, such as a blog, and online content of newspapers and magazines.

Therefore, the AVMS Directive replaces the notion of "television broadcasts" under the TVWF with the broader "audiovisual media services" which covers all commercial services which provide moving images in order to inform, entertain or educate (whether such services are "linear" or "non-linear"). The EC Commission intentionally excluded all forms of private correspondence, such as e-mails sent to a limited number of recipients, and services where the audiovisual content is merely ancillary to the provision of another service.

Linear and non-linear audiovisual media services

Article 1 of the AVMS classifies audiovisual media services into two categories which are treated differently under the AVMS. The first sub-category is referred to as "television broadcast" or "linear service". It covers audiovisual media services provided by a media service provider for simultaneous viewing of programmes on the basis of a programme schedule, including analogue and digital television, live streaming, webcasting and near-video-on-demand. The second sub-category includes "on-demand" or "non-linear services", which are provisions of audiovisual content "for the viewing of programmes at the moment chosen by the user and at his/her individual request on the basis of a catalogue of programmes selected by the media service provider".

Two-tier regulation

Under Art 1, audiovisual service providers are defined as the persons with editorial responsibility for the choice of content of the audiovisual media service (linear, non-linear or both) and who determine the manner in which content is organised. Nonetheless, linear audiovisual media services and non-linear audiovisual service providers are under different obligations, with the former subject to heavier regulation. A set of basic rules applies to all audiovisual media services and additional regulation applies only to television broadcasts (linear services). This different treatment is premised on the recognition that traditional television broadcasting is more influential and concerns a much broader user base than non-linear services which is more individualised as a result of users' individual choice of content.

During the consultation on the AVMS, one of the major concerns raised was against the potential application of AVMS to Internet services which might place undue regulatory burdens on delivery services. In view of its technical neutrality, the Commission clarifies that Internet service is outwith the scope of the AVMS provided that it does not contain Internet protocol television.

Articles 3a–3g of the AVMS Directive set forth the basic rules applicable to all audiovisual media services, whether linear or non-linear, as the following:

(1) *information requirements*: all audiovisual media service providers must make certain information available to recipients of their services in a form that is easily, directly and permanently accessible; this includes the name of the media service provider, the geographical address at which the media service provider is established, rapid contact details (such as an e-mail address) and details of any competent regulatory or supervising bodies;

(2) *protection of minors*: audiovisual media service providers must take appropriate measures to ensure that on-demand audiovisual media services which might seriously impair the physical, mental or moral development of minors are only made available in such a way that ensures that minors will not normally hear or see such services, as well as being encouraged to develop codes of conduct

regarding the advertising of junk food accompanying or included in children's programmes;

(3) *incitement to hatred*: audiovisual media services must not contain any incitement to hatred based on race, sex, religion or nationality;

(4) *disability*: audiovisual media services must be gradually made accessible to people with a visual or hearing disability;

(5) *rights holders*: audiovisual media services must not transmit cinematographic works outside periods agreed with rights holders;

(6) *editorial responsibility*: "editorial responsibility" means responsibility for the selection and organisation, on a professional basis, of the content of an audiovisual offer. This may apply to an individual content or a collection of contents. Such editorial responsibility applies to the composition of the schedule, in the case of television programmes, or to the programme listing, in the case of non-linear services.

(7) *sponsorship and/or product placement*: the AVMS Directive contains a number of rules relating to product placement (which will expressly be permitted for certain types of programme including cinematographic works, films, sports programmes and light entertainment programmes or where there is no payment but only the provision of certain goods or services free of charge, such as production props and prizes, with a view to their inclusion in a programme) and sponsorship:

  (i) the scheduling and content of audiovisual media services that have been sponsored or contain product placement may not be influenced in such a way as to affect the responsibility and editorial independence of the media service provider;

  (ii) sponsorship/product placement must not directly encourage the purchase or rental of goods or services in particular by making special promotional references to these goods or services;

  (iii) viewers must be clearly informed of the existence of a sponsorship agreement and/or the existence of product placement in an audiovisual media service;

  (iv) audiovisual media services must not be sponsored by undertakings whose principal activity is the manufacture or sale of cigarettes and other tobacco products and must not contain placement of tobacco products or cigarettes;

(v) the sponsorship of audiovisual media services by companies whose activities include the manufacture or sale of medicinal products and medical treatment may promote the name or image of the company, but may not promote specific medicinal products or medicinal treatments available only on prescription in the relevant European Member State;

(vi) news and current affairs programmes must not be sponsored;

(vii) audiovisual media services for children, documentaries and religious programmes must not contain product placement;

(viii) "audiovisual commercial communications" (ie moving images accompanying an audiovisual media service which is designed to promote third party goods or services, including, for example, product placement) must not:

(a) be surreptitious (ie they must be readily recognisable as such);

(b) use subliminal techniques;

(c) prejudice respect for human dignity, include or promote any discrimination based on sex, racial or ethnic origin, nationality, religion or belief, disability, age or sexual orientation, or encourage behaviour prejudicial to health or safety;

(d) encourage behaviour grossly prejudicial to the protection of the environment;

(e) relate to cigarettes or other tobacco products;

(f) be aimed specifically at minors if the communication relates to alcoholic beverages and shall not encourage consumption of such beverages; and

(g) cause moral or physical detriment to minors.

Apart from the above rules applying to all audiovisual services, the AVMS Directive also set forth an extra layer of rules for broadcasters (liner services), mainly with regard to television advertising and the quota for European works.

Advertising

The AVMS Directive scraps the daily quantitative restriction on the amount of television advertising that can be shown in any one day and also the rules specifying the amount of time between advertising breaks. Accordingly, audiovisual media service providers will have flexibility when they insert advertising breaks, but subject to an hourly limit of 12 minutes of advertising time per clock hour of transmission, provided that insertion of these advertising breaks does not prejudice the integrity of the programme.

Compared with those of the TVWF, apparently the rules on advertising under the AVMS are significantly relaxed, allowing television service providers to draw more advertising revenues. This is seen as the Commission's response to the broadcasters' appeal that in a new communications environment consumers should have more choices in content.

The above quantitative advertising rules apply to television broadcasting only, while quantitative rules that used to apply to television broadcasting now extend to all audiovisual media services, including both linear and non-linear services. To clarify the distinction between commercial and non-commercial audiovisual services, the AVMS prohibits the use of subliminal techniques. In general, the quantitative rules require that the substance of advertising must comply with the provisions on protection of minors, the ban on discrimination, the ban on tobacco advertising and the restrictions on medicine and alcohol advertising, with a view to maintaining high standards.

Product placement is a practice widely used in advertising and which integrates advertisement of products into television programmes. The AVMS Directive acknowledges the negative effects of product placement on consumers and prohibits any form of surreptitious advertising including product placement. Without any explicit reference to product placement, the AVMS Directive provides a principle of separating of programming and advertising which would include product placement. However, the AVMS Directive permits national authorities of the Member States to make exceptions to the ban on product placement in films and series made for audiovisual media services, sports programmes and light entertainment programmes, although certain conditions are made. All product placement is prohibited in news, current affairs, documentaries and children's programmes. The AVMS Directive retains the TVWF's provisions on sponsorship by distinguishing sponsorship from product placement based upon a recognition that sponsorship can be identified by viewers as they are normally declared in the programme whereas product placement normally is integrated into the programme and therefore cannot be easily singled out. In order to protect the interests of consumers, the AVMS further requires audiovisual media service providers to maintain editorial independence from any commercial interest and prohibits promotion of products in sponsorship. News and current affairs programmes may not be sponsored. Where a programme contains sponsorship, the Directive requires that this be clearly notified to viewers. Where the text explicitly covers television advertising, sponsorship and teleshopping, the Directive requires that new forms or new techniques of advertising such as interactive advertising, virtual advertising or split screen are compatible with the Directive.

Broadcasting rights to major events

In view of the significant social importance of major cultural and sports events for viewers, the TVWF required that the broadcast of certain events as determined by national authorities be accessible to the general public. The AVMS Directive retains the TVWF's provision in this regard, enabling Member States to compile a list of designated events which are regarded as being of major importance for society and prevents broadcasters from having exclusive rights to such events. The AVMS further introduces a provision on "short-reporting", giving any broadcaster established in the European Community access to short extracts of events of high interest to the public if such rights are held on an exclusive basis by a broadcaster in a Member State. However, the extracts can be used only in news and current affairs programmes on a fair, reasonable and non-discriminatory basis, and provided that the source of the extracts can be clearly identified.

European works

AVMS Directive retains the TVWF's requirement for the quota of the works of European origin in terms of dedicating time and budget. While it is acknowledged that the specific quotas originally set by the TVWF could not easily be applied to on-demand content, Art 3(h) of the AVMS Directive requires Member States to oblige on-demand service providers to promote the production of and access to European works. The extension of this rule to on-demand audiovisual media services is premised on an assumption that the new services have the potential partially to replace television broadcasting. The major criteria for European works are as following:

(a) works originating from Member States;

(b) works originating from European third States party to the European Convention on Transfrontier Television of the Council of Europe;

(c) works co-produced in the framework of agreements related to the audiovisual sector concluded between the European Community and third countries and fulfilling the conditions defined in each of these agreements.

Essential Facts

- Under the Treaty of Rome there was no specific reference to the EEC's jurisdiction over media matters. The ECJ established the EC's jurisdiction over the media in case law to the extent where the freedom to provide a service, the fundamental principle of the Treaty of Rome, was engaged.

- The TVWF Directive was introduced in response to restrictive national regulations on transfrontier broadcasting which undermined the freedom to provide services within the EC. It set up pan-EC standards on satellite broadcasting services and advertisement rules as well as the requirement for the protection of minors and consumers.

- Having replaced TVWF, AVMS is so far the major legal instrument of the EC dealing with media matters. It sets up a two-tier regulatory framework which imposes heavy regulation on traditional broadcasting/linear services and lighter regulation of non-scheduled/non-linear services. It contains the provisions on advertisement, product placement, sponsorship, protection of minors, exclusive broadcasting rights and quota for European audiovisual works.

INDEX